Stories of Perseverance:
Volume I

Stories of Perseverance: Volume I

First edition: March 2016

Table of Contents

Foreword

Every day we are barraged with negative news. You can't turn on the television or open a newspaper without seeing a negative story. Even social media—a place that should be safe for us to happily gather electronically with our friends—isn't immune from the horrors of that same dose of daily negativity.

One day, after seeing too many of these negative stories all at once, I realized I wanted to do something about it. I didn't want to feel powerless about the way the world seemed to obsess over negativity—I wanted to take matters into my own hands and make a difference. That's when I came up with the idea for *Stories of Perseverance*. I knew there were true heroes in the world who we could focus our time and energy honoring, and I wanted to hear *their* stories, not negative ones.

We all face seemingly insurmountable battles, but I knew from talking with my clients, friends, associates and family that there were real-life heroes we could celebrate. Instead of seeing only the negative and letting their struggles get the best of them, heroes choose to see the positive in those situations and persevere through difficult times. I wanted to hear how these heroes overcame their battles and emerged on top so you—and I—could be inspired to do the same.

My hope is that *Stories of Perseverance* will create a movement to a more uplifting and positive world and allow people to speak out about their struggles with an air of positivity. We can all learn so much from one another and with all the bad that goes on in the world, I think it helps us to take time to see the good. Ultimately, I hope others come forward and want to share their stories in the future. One story at a time, we **can** make a difference.

My Story of Perseverance

Dennis Postema

Perseverance helps everyone reach their goals, and it's a topic of great importance to me. Without it I don't know how I would have gotten through some especially difficult times in my life.

The year I turned 20 was one of the most difficult and important periods of my life. That year I was laid off for the first time. While the layoff was a big deal when it happened, I realized how minor it was when I later lost my 24-year-old brother in a car accident. *That* changed my life forever. My brother was my best friend, yet I didn't take the time to grieve his loss. Instead I tried to step up and be strong for my family. At the time, I had a mentor who had lost a son. He gave me some great advice; he said, "You can let this completely ruin your entire life, or you can grieve and then learn from the tragedy." This didn't make it easier, but the perspective helped. Nonetheless, burying myself and my emotions in my work kept me from much-needed sleep, which was the likely cause of my later health problems.

Threaded amongst the tragedy of this life-changing year were some triumphs. I landed the job of my dreams and, less than a year later, was promoted to a trainer, then manager. I might have thought that feat impossible, but it wasn't, which was how I discovered the only limits my life had were those I imposed upon myself.

When I was 23, I lost my dream job, just after a tragic fire in my parents' barn took the lives of eight horses, most of which had been in our family for at least 19 years. You can imagine the amount of mourning we experienced after having just lost my brother less than three years before. It was the same year I started my first company—a risky move that many did not support. I didn't allow their limits to apply to my life, however.

Between the ages of 25 and 27 I had some of my greatest business successes and deepest personal health problems. At 25, all of the sleep deprivation, stress and overworking finally caught up with me and I was diagnosed with ulcerative colitis, a disease that causes an inflammation of the large intestine. It's a painful condition that affects everything you do, and fatigue is a major symptom. One time I lost 55 pounds in a matter of two weeks. Another time I lost 58 pounds in two weeks. During a flare-up I would find myself using the restroom three times an hour.

Finally, after specialists did all they could, the only option to attempt to regain my quality of life was to undergo surgery. I had three surgeries at the Cleveland Clinic. During the first one, my colon was removed, and I had an ostomy bag for nine months. During the second surgery, surgeons rebuilt my colon out of my small intestine. In the final surgery, they tested my new J-pouch (or semi-colon, as I call it) and everything was fixed.

Then, in 2012, just three days after my honeymoon, I became so ill during an evening out that my wife and I had to rush to the closest hospital. I remember crawling in begging for help. About three hours later I was headed, once again, to Cleveland Clinic in an ambulance. They did a CAT scan and rushed me in for emergency surgery due to a bowel obstruction. This time, I was hospitalized for 10 days because my small intestine had wrapped around my liver, an almost lethal incident according to the doctors. If I hadn't been in the physical shape I was in, they probably would have lost me.

Even this wasn't enough to stop me from moving forward toward my ultimate goals. As I healed, I continued thriving professionally—releasing two books that would go on to become bestsellers on Amazon within just seven months of the emergency surgery.

Never did I use my health as an excuse to stop working toward my goals or to give up on them. I never accepted less than what I wanted simply because it was easier. Despite my health problems, I started a second company as an extension of the first— and I took this one national. I also graduated college—yes, I graduated college after starting two successful businesses and in spite of my hospitalizations, surgeries and health problems. How? Perseverance—a trait every single contributor to this book has and something I bet you have, or can develop, too!

The truth is, there will always be obstacles on your path to success. Some will be in the form of other people who shun or make fun of your dreams and goals. Some will be in the form of personal life events far beyond your control. However, these events—no matter how tragic or seemingly insurmountable—can only get in the way of what you achieve if you allow them the power to do so.

Despite my temporary setbacks, I've continued forward, persevering toward my ultimate goal—a goal I've since partially realized and still reach toward every day.

Recently, I met with my team to go over ideas about an upcoming project. While discussing the goals of the assignment, the hopeful outcome, and ways to incorporate my new ideas into the plan, one of my team members asked what kind of limitations I wanted to place on the project. Kidding around with him, I said I had no limits. None—and neither should the team.

Later that evening, I was thinking about the conversation and realized that when it comes to the work I do and what I feel my capabilities are, I'm actually not kidding when I say there are no limits. I truly feel I have no limitations hanging over me, restricting the reach of my utmost potential. No limits on what I am capable of and none on what I can accomplish.

Who's to say I should have limits? When Napoleon Hill wrote, "Whatever the mind can conceive and believe, it can achieve," in his famous book, *Think and Grow Rich*, he gave the world a concise version of the secret to success. By sharing it in a book, he was making sure it no longer stayed a secret, but an accessible strategy for everyone.

Yet still, with such a simple blueprint for success readily available, every day people limit themselves—their lives, their passions and their work. Rather than conceiving, believing and achieving, they take the wind from the sails of their own dreams. They truncate their potential before setting off on that initial exploration to discover its true borders.

The truth is, no matter what your burning desire—whether it's to be a great entrepreneur or invent something amazing—you can do it if you persevere and if you allow yourself to live without limiting your own potential.

What is your reality? What do you want to accomplish? Whatever you can imagine in your mind, no matter what it may be, that imagined vision represents the reality of what your limits are. Just as a painter would have a difficult time creating a work of art he couldn't imagine and see in his mind's eye, so too will you have a difficult time creating a future that you don't allow yourself the freedom to imagine.

Everyone has a story to tell about a time during which they persevered—even if they don't realize that's what they did. Through the stories shared in this book, you will hopefully recognize shared traits that can help you persevere in your own journey.

Dennis M. Postema, RFC, is a successful entrepreneur, best-selling author, coach, speaker and registered financial consultant. Dennis has taught clients, agents and associates how to find motivation and ascend psychological barriers to achieve success. His dedication to improving lives has led him to work with renowned motivational and self-help industry heavyweights such as Jack Canfield and Brian Tracy.

> *"Permanence, perseverance and persistence in spite of all obstacles, discouragements and impossibilities: it is this that in all things distinguishes the strong soul from the weak."*
> --Thomas Carlyle

Life's Journey

Deb Meyer

Life is a journey with various twists, turns, ups and downs. "Life happens—deal with it and move on" has been my philosophy over the past six years. My most recent twist on the journey began with a mammogram and lab work. Little did I know the routine physical would lead me to a fork in the road called cancer.

During the first phone call I received from the doctor's office, a voice on the other end of the line said, "Something has shown up on your mammogram, and we suggest you see a surgeon. We recommend a biopsy just to make sure." I had the biopsy in early November 2007. My initial thoughts were, *I can do this, and everything will come back fine.* Boy, was I wrong. On November 27, 2007, I received news that I had breast cancer. I honestly didn't know whether to scream, yell, cry, or throw something. I told myself, "Life happens, Deb. Deal with it and move on. You can handle this."

The first thing I did was reach out to other survivors to seek advice, wisdom, and hope. I also made the decision to meet with an oncologist immediately to seek advice and educate myself. My daughter and I visited a women's boutique to see what breast prostheses would look like. The boutique visit was very helpful. It opened up a whole new world I knew nothing about, and to be honest, it took me by surprise. The ladies were very helpful, encouraging, and kind.

I made the decision to have both breasts removed. This decision was mine and mine alone to make, and happily, I also had the support of my family. To this day, I do not regret this decision. I was determined I was not going to go through this again. To me, the advantages outweighed the disadvantages. The upside of this is that I can now have any size breast I desire.

I had the double mastectomy on December 11, 2007. My surgery went well with no complications, and my life took on a whole new meaning. I knew in my heart I was going to beat this cancer one way or another. I have way too much to live for, a daughter getting married, a son in college, and a husband whom I love dearly. I was fortunate in not having to take radiation or chemo, but I did have to take a drug called Tamoxifen for the subsequent five years.

Eventually, I decided not to have the reconstructive surgery done on my breasts. While that's my decision today, I can always change my mind and have the surgery later—but right now, I'd rather focus on being cancer-free.

In August 2008 my daughter and I made the commitment to share my story and help raise funds for research. We raised over $5,000 and participated in the Susan G. Komen three-day, sixty-mile walk in Chicago.

As I said, life's journey is full of ups and downs. In 2013, during a routine physical, I got a CT scan with dye and something showed up in my kidney. The words hit me like a ton of bricks: we need you to see a surgeon. Question, again, why? No way? This time I ended up seeing two different surgeons, and once again I was told I might have cancer, this time in my kidney.

In June 2013 I had a partial kidney removed, and yes, it came back as cancer. I can't explain how deeply this news hit me, and the emotions that, to this day, swell inside me. I believe I am a very strong person, but this surgery kicked my butt. It was the very first time I actually asked the question, "Why?"

After having two cancer diagnoses, I made the decision with the encouragement of my daughter to have the genetic testing done. I am happy to say that I do not carry the gene, a fact that gave me, and my family, peace of mind.

If I can leave you with one very important piece of advice, it is this: Early detection is the best prevention. Both my cancers were detected early, and I am still here traveling on my life journey, living with my own message: Life happens—deal with it and move on. I am moving on each and every day, willing to share my story, and enjoying my time with family (especially my grandchildren!) and friends.

Cancer is NOT a death sentence; it is just a side trip in your journey through life. I may not be done with this cancer journey, but I'm not willing to let it stop me in my tracks.

Debra Meyer, Cancer Survivor
2007 Breast Cancer
2013 Kidney Cancer

> *"If you are going through hell,*
> *keep going."*
> --Winston S. Churchill

The Journey Through Grief

Penny Knapp

Grief. If you are reading this, you are either well enough now to step forward in your journey through grief or are looking for help. Maybe that help is for someone you know, or maybe you simply have some interest in the journey of a survivor's loss after a suicide. Whatever your reasons, welcome to my journey through grief after my son Nicholas died by suicide at the age of twenty.

It was 6:15 Sunday morning when I awoke to the sound of voices downstairs. I sat up and listened for a moment. I didn't recognize the low, slow-speaking voices. No laughter, and no more than one voice could be heard at a time. I couldn't hear my husband's voice among the others.

I threw something over my nightgown and started down the creaky wooden stairs. As I approached the bottom step, I realized the visitors were not familiar to me and I walked quicker. When I reached the doorway

I saw the black uniform. Then it hit me: two police officers at my kitchen table. Why?

I asked my husband. "What are you doing talking to these people without me?" Larry looked at me, his eyes puzzled, and replied, "They are talking to me, but I don't know what they are saying!"

I looked at one of the officers; he immediately stood up and introduced himself and his partner. Then, he told me that my son Nicholas had jumped to his death.

I remember leaning on the chest freezer, feeling like something had entered my body, like an ice cube going through my veins. I had a hard time concentrating on what really had happened. That ice cube transformed into a serious overflow of boiling water that tingled throughout my whole body.

From that moment on, my life, *our* lives, would never be the same. There is no time for preparation because you don't know what to prepare for. People came, and people went. The phone rang; the dog needed to be fed. What time was it? Appointments? There were no appointments to think about or remember because I didn't know what was happening to my mind; my brain couldn't think. When would it stop? Would it go away, ever?

I recall thinking, "SOMEONE PLEASE HELP ME. I'M NOT SURE WHAT TO DO OR WHERE TO GO! WHO TOOK MY LIFE AND BROKE IT INTO A 1000-PIECE PUZZLE?"

"OK. I have to get control of things. Why must I cry so much? Did I eat? God, I'm so tired. Where is Larry? What are my daughters, Marsha and Melanie, doing?"

I wasn't sure if two days or three days had passed when I asked my daughter, "What day is it? Have I slept all this time?" I knew I had to have been awake sometime throughout the days, but I couldn't remember. My body just wanted to be normal again.

Bill, the funeral director, entered our home to discuss the arrangements. I didn't know what time of day it was, but did that matter, really? It's not like I needed to clean or straighten up the house for company. I had absolutely no ability to prepare a meal, because I wasn't even sure what my responsibilities were.

My brain felt like it was in pieces. No human being can make responsible decisions or even be responsible for herself when her brain is in pieces. Who should be responsible for me? I am the mom! I am in my forties!

My daughters seemed to have it all under control. They spoke with Bill about the songs, the pictures they wanted to use. They designed a bookmark for all the people who visited the funeral home. I mentioned that I wanted Nicholas to be cremated. Then, it was decided; Nicholas' cowboy boots would hold his ashes.

Nicholas was such a cowboy. His cowboy hats, his boots, his belt buckles. Then, the thought hit me, what do I do with all his stuff? His room is full of his stuff, his belongings. This is all I have left of my twenty-year-old son.

I couldn't think. At times, I couldn't stop the tears. I didn't like feeling so sad and hurt and feeling the pain of the loss of my son. The thought of the loss by suicide was so unbearable. Thoughts like, WHY? What must he have been feeling to plan and carry out his death? Where was I? I'm sure I didn't miss something. I'm afraid to remember too hard in case I recall something important, like, what if he asked me for help? Did I know that and forget to help him? Was I supposed to have seen something? Nicholas, I am sorry I don't know if I wasn't there for you!

Two full days after I was told my son would never come home, my mind cleared somewhat, and I could think again. It was a double-edged sword; I realized I would never hear his voice again. I would never hear, "Pen, get a life!" I would not hear him tell me a humorous story and laugh. Now, I would have the bathroom to myself and no one else to share it with. I would never again clean up his mess in the kitchen. I wondered, did I complain too much and it upset him? Did I say something I shouldn't have before

Nicholas left the house that day? WHY can't I remember? Why? Why? Why?

The first two weeks felt like something else was inside my body giving me directions and keeping me alive. I couldn't do anything on my own. Someone must have put batteries in me, and that's what kept me moving, walking, and talking. My body was physically present, but my mind was everywhere, out there in the universe.

Eventually, things slowed down. People stopped coming around. The phone stopped ringing. Every time I looked out the front door window, Nicholas' four-wheel Jimmy sat facing the house like it was confused. What do I do with his truck? I went to the hardware store and bought a huge "For Sale" sign. I put it in the back window. Two weeks passed, and no one called or inquired.

When a person commits suicide, life feels like it's on pause for all those who loved the now-gone person. However, the earth still rotates, bills still come, and paperwork waits to be completed. I made phone calls regarding Nicholas' income tax and canceled his Social Security card, driver's license, and bank account. One day, while in Nick's room, I was standing in a daze and heard the sound of a cell phone ring. It broke through the fog, and I turned around to find it on the shelf next to Nick's wallet and truck keys. I hesitated for a minute but something inside reached out and picked up the phone. Reluctantly, I answered. "Hello?"

A soft, quivering female voice replied, "Oh, hi. I'm sorry. I just wanted to call and hear Nick's voice on his answering service."

"Hi, I'm Nick's mom. Please call back, and I won't answer this time." A few seconds passed before the phone rang again. I stood and thought about that poor girl, listening to her friend's voice to get some comfort while she grieved his loss.

For a while, Larry and I found it difficult to move on with our lives. We would receive the odd phone call from a family member requesting we come for dinner, and we always turned them down. We didn't feel like leaving our house. Our good friends invited us to a fiftieth birthday party, but we couldn't bring ourselves to attend. A family member called one time insisting we come for dinner. They pushed and said, "You never come over anymore, and we really want you to. Tell me you will come, or I will be hurt." I told them we'd come, but we never showed up.

It must've been three months after Nick's death when my eldest daughter said she wanted to hold a golf tournament in his memory. We did it and had a phenomenal event. It was an emotional event for the family and friends who attended and helped, but also a very healing one.

The journey through grief is long, but it evolves. Eventually, I reached a point where the pain compelled me into action. That's when I began my mission to work with Survivors of Suicide. Seeking knowledge and research information, I found helpful books and went to conferences with my daughter in the city. We attended everything available and met lots of people, networked, and gave our name and email to all of them.

However, I wanted to do more. I wanted to have my own group and my own resources to provide to others going through the same journey and, perhaps, to prevent another young person from taking his or her own life.

Our plans began with suicide awareness products. We found a company that was reasonably priced. Then, we had to market them. Let the survivors know they are not alone. They don't need to be alone. We formed a suicide committee with a couple of high school students and a youth group organizer. We began plans for our first suicide awareness walk.

I've met so many people who have been impacted by suicide that I wondered how I had come this far in life and never known these people before I'd faced my own experience.

I found a drive to survive the loss of my dear son Nicholas. Three and a half years later, I still have that drive and determination to survive my journey through grief. The only difference now is that I am determined to help other survivors of suicide loss, so they can also choose to live life again after their own tragedies.

Penny Knapp is determined to help other survivors of suicide loss so they will also choose to live life again after their most tragic loss. Visit her website http://rememberingnicholas.ca/Grief.html or her Facebook page facebook.com/SurvivorsOfSuicideLossNicholasKnapp

"You may encounter many defeats, but you must not be defeated.
In fact, it may be necessary to encounter the defeats, so you can know who you are, what you can rise from, how you can still come out of it."
--Maya Angelou

Living with Moyamoya

Tiffany Tosh

My name is Tiffany Tosh. I am 46 years old, and I have degrees in chemistry and medical technology. For 16 years I worked in a hospital laboratory, first as an MT generalist and finally as a chemistry specialist. I was married and in the process of a divorce when I got sick. My greatest loves are my pets. At the time I got sick, I had three cats and two dogs, but I had to give them away.

I was also an artist. I painted watercolors, mostly portraits and landscapes, but around Christmas 2008, I started painting ornaments in watercolor. I made quite a bit of money from that, but since suffering a stroke, I can no longer paint. Now, I mostly read or play games on my iPad. I do laundry and help my mom clean the house. I want to work but have not been able to find a job.

In 2009, I was diagnosed with Moyamoya disease, caused by the spontaneous occlusion of the circle of Willis, a system of arteries that feeds blood to the brain. Basically, this means the vessels that carry blood to my brain closed off, which often causes strokes and death. There is no cure, and the disease is progressive. I learned I had it after I started having ministrokes and underwent an MRI. Luckily, the radiologist reading the scans knew what it was and sent me immediately to the emergency room.

I had two surgeries to essentially bypass the blood flow to the brain. The first surgery went well. It was on the left side of my brain because the ministrokes were on that side, causing paralysis on the right side. The second surgery went well too, but the day after surgery, the nurse asked if I wanted to sit up in a chair to eat breakfast. When they moved me into a chair, sitting up caused my blood pressure to drop precipitously so the blood wasn't even reaching my brain. This caused a massive stroke, and I almost died.

I spent 13 days in ICU. I regained consciousness on the third day and everybody was so excited. Unfortunately, I didn't recognize the left side of my body. It was as if I didn't even have a left side. I didn't speak or act like I recognized anyone. My mom was worried that she'd never hear me call her Mama again.

Eventually I started speaking, though not clearly. I was transferred back to Jackson, Tennessee, for inpatient rehabilitation. I was there for 21 days. It was hard work, but I learned to talk, walk and think all over again. My therapists were exceptional. They all worked hard to make sure I was able to function. I am truly blessed by God for wonderful parents, awesome friends and great therapists.

> *"Even if I knew that tomorrow the world*
> *would go to pieces,*
> *I would still plant my apple tree."*
> --Martin Luther

Kicking Cancer's Butt

Anna Cheek

My name is Anna Cheek, and I am the mother of Ali, one of the strongest, most beautiful young ladies you will ever meet; not that I'm biased or anything. This is the story of everything she has undergone in her short childhood. She has chosen to block out a lot of the bad memories and heart wrenching obstacles she's endured. Ali's father, Derek, and I are okay with that. We don't want her childhood to be memories of hospital stays, surgeries, and sickness. Although Ali will never forget what has happened to her, she does know what it means to be a fighter. In this fight, she has chosen which situations she needs to remember to help her be a stronger person in life.

It all started when Ali was only 19 months old. She woke up one morning screaming her head off. Her dad handed her to me, hoping I could do something. When I took her, she passed out right in my arms. Ali's doctor told us to bring her right over. When we got there, the staff was waiting for us at the back door. Dr. McClarren took one look at Ali and said, "I can call a rescue squad and you can ride with me, or you can take her, but we've got to get her to the hospital immediately."

When we got to the hospital, her vitals were very low, and they couldn't figure out why. She had oxygen on and wires attached everywhere on her body. After a CT scan, we went back to the ER. I knew something wasn't right. Dr. McClarren came out and told me Life Flight was on its way. I asked her if Ali was going to make it. With tears in her eyes, Dr. McClarren replied, "I can't answer that right now."

Ali still had not regained consciousness by the time Life Flight arrived, but as they loaded her onto the helicopter, her eyes opened. By the time I arrived at the ICU at Toledo Children's Hospital, I could hear her screaming. When I entered her room, she yelled, "Mommy!" It was the best sound in the world.

The doctors never did find a reason for this terrible episode.

When Ali was seven, she told me one afternoon that she wanted to show me a magic trick she learned at school. She took a quarter in her hand and popped it in her mouth. She then stared at me, doing nothing. I very calmly asked her if she'd swallowed the quarter. With her eyes as wide as could be, she shook her head yes. I then panicked and started beating her back and sticking my finger down her throat. Having no success, I took her to the hospital where they took an X-ray, which showed that the quarter was lodged in her throat. She underwent surgery within minutes to have it removed. I was told if the quarter tilted just a hair, it could cut off her airway and to remove it was tricky. If it hadn't come out smoothly, it could've torn her esophagus or trachea, so they had Life Flight on standby.

Just before Ali's eighth birthday, she was complaining of stomach pains. We took her to the doctor, but they couldn't find anything. They thought maybe she was lactose intolerant. A week later she was crawling down the stairs crying. Her appendix was leaking and about to burst. They transferred Ali to Toledo Children's Hospital. She underwent surgery that evening and had to stay in the hospital for a few days because the poison from her appendix leaked into her system. They had to keep an eye on her and give her lots of antibiotics.

As difficult, painful, and scary as each of those incidents was, no part of Ali's journey compares to what happened next. It was early March 2006. A cold sore had developed underneath Ali's nose. Since I am prone to them, I didn't think it was any big deal, but it would not heal. She then got a few more on her lips. I decided to take her to the doctor. They gave her a strong antibiotic and told us that if it didn't get better, they would try an immune therapy on her. It took a good two weeks, but the sores finally started to heal. Ali still seemed weak, always watching television and lying around with hardly any energy. I called the doctor's office, and they decided to try another antibiotic. I felt in my heart something just wasn't right, but you listen to the doctor's opinion.

April 6, 2006, our lives changed forever. I was at school helping another class when Ms. Foltz, Ali's teacher, came and got me. She asked me to come take a look at Ali because she just wasn't her usual outgoing self. I peeked in and saw that Ali was sleeping on her desk. When I went to her desk, Ali looked up at me with the most pitiful eyes and gray-colored skin I have ever seen. I called her doctor and demanded they do a blood test to see if anything was going on. They told me to take her to the hospital and have some blood work done.

Instead of making us wait days for the results, a nurse said our doctor wanted us to go right over to her office. When I saw Dr. McClarren's face, I knew something was wrong. She only made eye contact with Ali and asked her, "Do you know what cancer is?"

My heart dropped. Ali answered, "Yes. I just finished the Math-a-thon for St. Jude."

The doctor explained what was going to happen. I couldn't hear anything she was saying. She'd just told me my baby had cancer.

****

It was a whirlwind after that. We were immediately sent to Toledo Children's Hospital. Early the next morning, Ali was taken into surgery for her first bone marrow biopsy. This confirmed the diagnosis. Ali had acute lymphoblastic leukemia, the T-cell form. If you were to have leukemia, this was the good one to have. Even though they tell you that, it doesn't make you feel any better.

On her third day there, Ali was to have a port put in. This is a device installed into the chest area so a line can be run direct to a vein. This makes it easier to have an IV put in multiple times. We went with Ali down to the operating room, but when they checked her temperature, it was 105.7 degrees, so they could not do the surgery, and they had to work to get her temp down. Ali was happy, though, because she didn't want to have surgery. That is one thing she remembers. They eventually got the fever down and installed her port.

She then started a protocol treatment that my husband and I chose. It was a hard choice. You hope you're picking the right one. What if you pick the wrong one, and it doesn't work? We decided to go with a protocol that we researched to be the best. Ali's uncle Chad had also been diagnosed with ALL when he was little. Chad's mom told us he had been a test subject for this protocol, and it worked. There were a few things that were tweaked but it was, for the most part, the same. It was a treatment regimen that would entail approximately four bone marrow biopsies and 20 lumbar punctures—the chemotherapy medicine would be put directly into the spine. Ali had chemo for two years and two months—the frequency varied from every day, a few times a week, once a week, and for the last year, once a month, along with lots and lots of pills.

Only eight years old, her life was altered more than anyone could imagine. She went from playing softball and being outside all day to sitting either in a hospital room or secluded at our house. If the blood work showed that her numbers were down, she wasn't allowed to have contact with too many people. Everyone had to use a lot of sanitizer around her. She missed over 90 days of school in the fourth grade. For two years, she was not allowed to sleep over at any of her friends' homes because she had to take from seven to 30 pills every night. There is no liquid form for these pills, which made it challenging. Some of them were tiny but some were just way too big for a little girl to take. Sometimes we would sit there for hours trying to get them all down.

I had to go on every school trip with her, for my peace of mind and for the school's. I think Ali's situation made everyone a little uncomfortable. Who could blame them? She still tried anything she could. She was the strong one. I cried my heart out. I didn't want her to have to deal with any more heartbreak than she already had.

One of the most heartbreaking things Ali had to deal with happened at the mall in Fort Wayne. She had gotten some gift cards for her birthday and wanted to use them. Everyone from our area was very supportive of her, so she was comfortable not wearing a wig or other head covering. So comfortable, we didn't think twice when we headed to the mall. We'd just come down the escalator to the food court and an older couple was going up the escalator. They couldn't take their eyes off her. We were used to people looking or doing a double take, but this became uncomfortable when the couple came back down and circled our area numerous times. Ali was getting noticeably upset, asking why they would be doing that. I tried to reassure her that they didn't mean any harm. As we walked away, I smiled at them and politely said, "Yes, she has cancer, but she is doing great. Thank you."

****

The illness and chemotherapy compromised Ali's immune system. Every time she got a slight fever, it would turn into at least a three-day stay at the hospital. This happened quite a bit. When you're at the hospital this much, you come to have a second family: the doctors, nurses, staff, and the rest of the families who are going through the same thing. It becomes a close-knit little community.

During one long stay at the hospital, Ali's favorite nurse, Laura, was giving Ali a blood transfusion and chemo. The staff was always good about explaining everything that could or would happen. Laura was explaining to Ali that the medicine would make her hair fall out, either a little at a time or in big chunks. Ali started bawling. "No one told me I was going to lose my hair," she stated in a very serious voice. She finally came to terms with it. That was the first and only time she cried about having cancer.

On November 20, 2011, we lost a dear friend and fellow cancer patient, Tiana, to the fight against the disease. It was a very emotional time for Ali. Before we went into the showing, we sat in the car as she cried. We discussed why her emotions were getting the best of her. Ali said, "On one hand, I'm so thankful that you, Dad, and Taylor never had to go through this pain. I am happy I get to experience life. But Mom, I feel guilty that I'm here and she is not. I don't want her parents to be upset when they see me because I get to be here and Tiana doesn't." When we entered the viewing, Tiana's mom grabbed Ali and hugged and hugged and hugged her. They both cried. Ali knew they weren't upset with her, but it didn't make the guilt any easier, she said.

****

It's interesting to discover the things that Ali has chosen to remember. She remembers taking some medicine that made her a little — well, a lot — mean. Ali also remembers being sick after treatments or having to have pillowcases put over the bag of blood during transfusions so she wouldn't get sick looking at it.

One of her best memories is of her trip to the Bahamas for Make-a-Wish—from the limo to her first ride in a plane to the Atlantis Hotel and the waterpark. Ali remembers swimming with the dolphins and also meeting the Jonas Brothers (as she would say, "Back when they were cool"). To my husband and me, that trip was bittersweet. It was awesome to see how much fun she had but the reason we took the trip wasn't so much fun.

Ali also remembers getting Olive Garden soup after every treatment. They got to know us by name there. It was the only thing she could eat. We would buy it by the gallon because she ate so much.

Something Ali takes with her to this day is a bit of a germ phobia. She's getting better, she says, but still has her moments. She's an active, happy girl, and we couldn't be more proud. She loves volleyball and has made every team from junior high on. The volleyball program does a game night called

Volley for a Cure. In previous years, they recognized her at the games and she smiled and was polite. Well, things change; she grew up and finally realized she had something to be proud of. She kicked cancer's butt. So, when the varsity coach recognized Ali this time, she felt something different. She cried and cried and cried. I didn't see her for a little bit, so I went to see if she was okay. I met her in the hall where she ran to me, hugged me, and said, "What is wrong with me?" I told her, "Absolutely nothing. You are perfect."

Ali has persevered through one of the most difficult things there is to overcome. She now wants to help spread awareness about cancer and finding a cure. Even though she is still a little shy, she joins in as much as she comfortably can. Her confidence is coming along, which has taken a long time. She's living life to the fullest. Who could ask for anything more?

> *"Always bear in mind that your own resolution to succeed is more important than any one thing."*
> --Abraham Lincoln

Writing Saved My Life

Felicia

My second grade teacher, Ms. Medley, gave me my first writing assignment: one paragraph about something that I wanted. I titled the assignment, *I Want a Dog.* Paragraph one started with how much I would have liked to have a dog (very much), why (because they are so cute and fluffy), and the reason I couldn't have one (our home was too small). When I finished writing the reason I couldn't have a dog, I began a second paragraph, then a third and a fourth. By the time I ran out of paper, I had written 100 pages.

Monday morning came and Ms. Medley read a few students' paragraphs aloud. When she finally got to mine, she held my notebook up and said, "Felicia has written a novel! It is called *I Want a Dog.*"

After school, Ms. Medley took the time to explain that a novel is a prose narrative made up of characters, emotions, and expressions. She told me that writers who produce these novels are called authors. Ms. Medley said that if I kept writing, one day I could be an author.

I asked her if I was in trouble for doing the assignment incorrectly. Ms. Medley's reply was not what I'd expected. She said, "Felicia, the assignment was completed correctly as long as it was written by you and you feel that everything you want to express is in the story." I said it was, and she replied, "Okay. You're a writer. Keep on writing." I never forgot Ms. Medley's encouraging words, and I've kept on writing ever since. Writing has helped me throughout my life.

Growing up, I suffered from child abuse and depression. My parents had me when they were very young, and my mother was single for the majority of my teenage years. As the oldest of my mother's four children, I took on a lot of responsibility, caring for my brothers and sister. Growing up fast had its consequences. I developed major depression and was put on medication and saw a therapist. However, I found that writing was the best therapy.

When I was fifteen years old, I met a young lady named Holly during one of my group therapy sessions for child-abuse survivors. She and I had a lot in common. Not only were we both survivors of abuse, we both suffered from depression. Holly was diagnosed with borderline personality disorder (BPD).

Holly was the kind of friend I'd always wanted. She was kind, thoughtful, and a very good listener. We had a brief friendship, but in that short time, she gave me a lifetime of wonderful memories that I'll never forget. My friend lost her battle with BPD and committed suicide when she was only fifteen years old. For years, I kept journals and wrote about things, like my memories of Holly and what it was like growing up. Before I realized it, the journals had turned into a novel of great memories.

Years after Holly's death, I had an idea to write a story about a girl who'd suffered from depression and BPD, but survived all that she had been through. I started on a story with Holly in mind and combined a bit of what it was like growing up for me and surviving my own experiences.

I knew that if I continued down the path of healing, I would be able to help others who had suffered from child abuse and mental illness. Therefore, I continued to write and eventually produced my first novel called *Her*. *Her* is a story of hope and survival.

I use writing and speaking to help people and family members of those who have suffered abuse and mental illness. I share my story to help others instead of using it as an excuse to not accomplish my goals and move forward in life.

I'm a youth advocate, mentor, and behavioral health worker. I speak out against child abuse and work to raise awareness about mental illness, particularly personality disorders. As a mentor, I've helped youths transition from inpatient treatment to living an independent life outside of the hospital. I've helped them prepare for job interviews, pay their own bills, and apply for college. I've seen many youths who struggle with mental illness transition from being completely dependent on the system to gaining their independence and living on their own.

I'll never forget the first time Ms. Medley told me what an author was. From that moment, I knew that was my calling. Writing *is* my life because writing *saved* my life. I don't only write for myself, but I write for others. I try to always write with a purpose. It is as Maya Angelou said:

"I've learned that people will forget what you said, people will forget what you did, but people will never forget how you made them feel."

Like Angelou, I write to make my readers feel.

I can honestly say that writing saved my life. I will continue to write and encourage others to speak up through journaling, writing, and raising awareness of child abuse and mental illness.

> *"Nothing in the world can take the place of persistence. Talent will not: nothing is more common than unsuccessful men with talent. Genius will not; unrewarded genius is almost a proverb. Education alone will not; the world is full of educated derelicts. Persistence and determination alone are omnipotent."*
> --Calvin Coolidge

Determined to Break the Mold

Travis

My name is Travis. I am 33 years old and have been married for two years to my amazing wife, Kate. I have a master's degree in education and have taught biology for the past 10 years. For the past six years, I've been the head coach of a high school football team. I have no children, other than the students I coach and teach each year.

I was born in a small, rural town in 1979 to two high school students who had an unplanned pregnancy. My dad was just 18, my mom only 17. From the beginning, this wasn't an ideal situation to bring a child into, but my parents were determined to do everything in their power to make sure I had everything a child needed to achieve his dreams. Money and resources were minimal at best, but they both worked full-time jobs to put food on the table. Dad began working at a local factory and Mom worked odd jobs until I was old enough to go to a babysitter, at which time my mom worked at various factories in town. I had a great childhood with more love than I could ask for. I have very fond memories of my childhood—of time spent fishing and having family get-togethers where stories and laughs were plentiful. I remember feeling so happy.

Once I started school, my eyes were opened wide to a part of the world I never knew existed. There were kids with in-ground pools, brand new cars, huge houses, four-wheelers, arcades in their basements, brand new Nikes, and other expensive material items I didn't have. I became self-conscious that I wasn't ever going to fit in with that crowd. I was a very anxious child and worried about miniscule things to the point that it would make me sick.

My parents were aware of my insecurities about our financial situation and did everything to make sure I had the "cool" shoes and clothes for school. In order to give me these things, they took overtime at work whenever they could get it and made many personal sacrifices. Looking back, I feel very selfish about the things I classified as "needs," because it meant my parents had to buy their clothes at the thrift store and go months upon months without haircuts and other niceties. They worked their fingers to the bone just to have the bare necessities while making sure I would fit in. Still, what we lacked in money, my parents made up for in love. I was a mama's boy and Dad's sidekick. Life was good.

The Fire Is Lit

As I grew older and progressed through school, I learned just how difficult life was for my parents working in their respective factories. My parents had always told me how smart and athletic I was and always believed I would be something special. True to form, I was a fast runner and excelled in sports. I made every all-star team and was always one of the first kids picked in gym class. Not to let the intellectual side slide, I was in the gifted class in school.

I can't pinpoint when it happened, but this was when I first started to think about that age-old question, "What do I want to be when I grow up?" Having seen how rough my parents' day-to-day lives were and how early they had to grow up with my unexpected arrival, I knew I didn't want that. My parents didn't want that for me, either. However, I wasn't sure how I could possibly take a different path and go to college to be a professional.

No one in my family or extended family had gone to college. Everyone was a grinder. They were all blue-collar workers, and the conversations at parties revolved around their hatred of their jobs. A few had aspirations of going to college; some had even tried it. None had made it. My parents laid the foundation for me to change all of that. They lived vicariously through me. They were stern and placed high expectations on me, but always tempered these sentiments with unwavering support and love. The fire was lit. I was determined to break the mold.

High School

By high school, I'd completely fallen in love with sports. Football, baseball and basketball occupied most of my daily thoughts. Football, however, quickly became my passion. I was able to earn my varsity letter as a freshman. As a sophomore, I was a starter and earned all-league honors. As a junior, I was a starter on both offense and defense, again earning all-league honors. As a senior, I was voted team captain and had a season that made me well known in our little community. I earned first-team all-league honors on offense and defense. I was named to the Four County All-Star team. With 29 touchdowns, an 11.1 yards per carry and a career average of 8.9 yards per carry, I broke the school records. Recruiting letters from smaller schools flooded our mailbox. I realized then that football could possibly be my path to college. Academics never took a backseat to football—my parents and coaches would have never let that happen. I was one of the smart kids in my class, and that was the path to college that I had more control over.

My parents could see I was approaching that pivotal point where I'd need to make some big decisions. College was the only option, but I had no idea how I could go if I couldn't pay for it. I knew my parents didn't have a college fund for me, and they couldn't afford loans to get me through. What was I going to do?

After my senior season of football, I decided that I didn't care if I had to take out $100,000 in loans in my own name, I was going to break the mold. I was going to go to college and FINISH. Graduation came, and I'd enrolled in a small, private college about an hour and a half from home. There, not only would I further my education, but I'd continue with my passion—football.

College

During my first year in the dorm, as I took the step only a few in my family had attempted, I questioned myself over and over. I kept thinking that I'd already earned my high school diploma; why not just get a job as a full-time grinder? But my parents were not going to let that happen. I'd come too far. They told me I was destined for better than they had. Not wanting to disappoint, I pushed on—and not just academically. I can still see the look of pride on my dad's face the day he found out that I lettered as a freshman cornerback on a Division III college football team. He was proud of his boy, and that further fueled my fire to finish this step in my life.

The next few years brought on changes in colleges and majors. In spring 2003 I graduated magna cum laude with a degree in life science education. I've never seen my mom as happy as she was on that warm, May day. She, along with my little brother, beamed with pride. Her son had beaten the odds. Together, <u>we</u> had changed the path of my life. No one could've known that when two high school kids had a baby in the fall of 1979, they weren't just bringing life into the world—they were breaking the cycle.

The Message

After graduation, I immediately got a job teaching high school biology, coaching baseball and my beloved football. However, my education wasn't over. Next step: push the bar higher. What about a master's degree? Absolutely! Winter 2007, I earned my master's degree in education.

Perseverance is the trait that got me to that point, but it didn't come solely from within me. It came from within *us*. My mom, my dad, and my brother. Now when I walk into my classroom each year, there are 125 young people who probably have stories similar to mine. So many doubts. So many limitations. So many hurdles. Some of those students don't have parents who encourage them to break the mold, to form their own path and not let the decisions and outcomes of their parents dictate their future. I tell my story. I let them know that being poor, living in a mobile home, not having the "cool" clothes, not having the perfect, cookie-cutter life doesn't dictate their future. For every person out there who gives you reasons you can't do something, there is another who will prove to you that you *can* do whatever you want. Just believe. Life is good.

Travis Cooper attended Fairview High School. Upon graduation he played football at Ohio Northern University before graduating Magna Cum Laude from Defiance College with a bachelor's degree in life science education. After completing his undergraduate degree, Travis completed his master's degree from Marygrove College in Detroit. He is currently a high school biology teacher at Wauseon High School and the head football coach. In his free time Travis loves to travel. He lives in Defiance, OH with his wife Kate and dog, Bear.

> *"Courage is not the absence of fear,*
> *but the triumph over it."*
> --Nelson Mandela

The Terrible Diagnosis

Eesha Gogia

I am Eesha Gogia. In the latter part of the 1990s, I began having peculiar health problems, like falling for no reason, but I did not take it seriously. By early 1999, when I was just twenty-five and two years into my marriage, the symptoms became alarmingly severe. I started losing my balance while walking and could no longer leave the house. My vision was distorted, making it totally black out. The doctors said that it was multiple sclerosis. We were devastated, and I did not want to accept the terrible diagnosis.

In December 1999, my husband, Girish, took me to Goa for a holiday. While there he had a terrible accident, which left him paralyzed from the neck down due to spinal injury. I was left to struggle with my growing MS impairment while tending to my husband. I soon realized my limbs were not functioning, and it was a brain-related problem. In spite of all this, I still took care of my husband, dealing with his physical issues, including an aggressive bedsore. Eventually, it became very difficult for me to take care of him and also do my daily chores.

By 2006, my condition had worsened. I could barely walk, and often moved forward by dragging my legs. I gradually realized it would be difficult for my elderly in-laws to take care of two bedridden people. I prayed for understanding and decided it would be best for me to go back to my parents' house. During this time, one of my lowest points, a family friend introduced me to Nichiren Buddhism, which is based on the writing of Nichiren Dashonin. I took up the practice, praying sincerely for my husband. The prayer gave me the courage to understand our sicknesses, and I refused to be defeated.

My family welcomed me back on December 15, 2006, supporting me wholeheartedly despite the upheaval to their lives. Soon, however, my legs stopped moving, and my lower body became immobile. I was no longer able to take care of myself. I was catheterized. I became absolutely bedridden. My friends initially took me for outings in a wheelchair; once that became difficult, they continuously met me at home.

In January 2010, my husband and I both went for stem cell therapy and stayed in the same hospital room for five days. It was our first time together after a very long time apart! The therapy was not a success, but it brought us together. We are now able to meet sometimes when Girish comes home in his wheelchair.

We celebrated his birthday together with his school friends. It was a happy and touching time in my life. Before his birthday, I would cry a lot, feeling very sad for myself. I could not control my tears. Now, a smile is kind of stuck on my face. Today at the age of thirty-eight, my spirit is always high, and I take my situation in stride. I pray rather than bemoan my situation.

Thanks to the practice of Buddhism that I have taken up, I have enough courage to face each day joyfully with my family and my GAKKAI members. I used to find it difficult to chant as breathlessness affected my voice. My fellow GAKKAI members refused to allow me to slip into defeat. **Buddhism is about winning**. The women's division campaign has been absolutely joyous for me. I was a speaker and spoke extempore. After many months, I dressed in beautiful formal clothes and took part in the dance, sitting where I was and sharing fully in the happy experience. My joy knows no bounds when my fellow GAKKAI members say that every time they meet me, they are so encouraged.

I am praying and looking forward to many more of these moments. My only wish is to go back to walking to my husband's house so I can live happily with him.

"Life is not easy for any of us.
But what of that? We must have
perseverance and above all confidence in
ourselves. We must believe that we are
gifted for something and that this thing
must be attained"
--Marie Curie

The Results Are In

Sherry

There are times in our lives when our strength, resolve, and faith are tested. We may not be able to see this at the time, but God has a plan for our lives. Sometimes finding out how strong you truly are is a hard road to follow, but you never know what you are capable of without taking the path. My name is Sherry, and I would like to share my journey with you.

"You have breast cancer." Those four words turned my world upside down. Suddenly, my vision of a fun, peaceful summer relaxing and spending time at the beach turned into doctor appointments, tests, scans, and chemotherapy. Instead of reading a novel or two, I was reading test results, pamphlets, booklets, and articles about breast cancer and the side effects of chemo. As odd as it sounds, the words that really rocked my world were, "You will lose your hair."

The lump was large and the cancer aggressive, so I had to begin chemotherapy as quickly as possible. Soon there was a plan, and the routine took shape. Strong chemo every other Friday followed by a shot of Neulasta on Monday, aches, pains, and tears on Wednesday. By the Wednesday following my "off" week, I began to feel good … just in time to do it all over again on Friday.

The doctor told me I would begin to lose my hair within fourteen days. On day thirteen, it started coming out in clumps. I tried to spare it and hid the thinning under scarves for a couple of days but finally it got to be too much. When I got home from work I began cutting my hair with the intent of shaving off the last bits. By divine intervention, my husband did not have to work late, and he took on that task. It was traumatic for both of us, a moment we will never forget. We were in this together.

During these treatments I experienced leg swelling and rapid heart rates that were very scary. By the end of the first eight weeks, the combination of treatment and working full-time left me running on empty. Then, one day, I drove to work and passed out in my car in the parking lot. I was taken to the hospital where it was discovered I had an infection. I was started on a course of strong, broad-based antibiotics. I was in the hospital for three days and was able to go home only to return two days later with a very high fever.

The antibiotics caused a digestive disorder called C. diff, and I was hospitalized for eight more days. I was confined to my room and anyone who entered had to wear a gown and gloves. It was not a good experience at all. After twenty-four hours of no fever, I was able to go home. I could not believe how weak I had grown over that two-week period. I could barely walk from my room to the elevator but there was a spring in my step—I was going home.

The illness set my treatment plan back two weeks but I was finally able to begin phase II. Now, my body would face two new drugs every week for twelve weeks and a whole new set of side effects. Things seemed to be going well and the tumor had shrunk considerably. However, with the good came the bad, and I soon realized there was numbness in my toes and fingers. The doctor was concerned about the neuropathy and interrupted the treatments to schedule surgery.

During this whole ordeal, my family, friends, church, and people across the country were praying for God's healing. I know God was always with me because no matter how bad I felt, it could have been much worse. As a breast cancer patient, you know an operation is in your future, but you don't know how invasive it will be. The cancer was in my right breast and the lymph nodes under that arm. There is always an element of fear that the cancer will return, no matter what course of treatment you follow. My husband and I decided that I was going to have a mastectomy, no matter what, in hopes of eliminating that possibility.

At our appointment, the surgeon shared how pleased she was with the results of the chemotherapy. My very large tumor that would have required a mastectomy to be removed was now so small she had to use an ultrasound to locate it. After discussing my options with my doctor, I decided to have a lumpectomy, a considerably less invasive surgery. It was time to honor all the prayers and put my faith in what God had done. Surgery was scheduled and that day we were doubly blessed. Only a small portion of the breast had to be removed with some lymph nodes. All tests on the tissue returned clear. I was cancer-free. Even the lymph nodes that had previously tested positive were now negative. And the second blessing that day, our grandson was born.

Although the results of the tests were very good, it was still recommended that I complete the treatments that had been interrupted and follow them with radiation therapy. Following this course of treatment would give me the best possible odds of remaining cancer-free, and I was all for that. After six more weeks of chemo, the numbness in my toes and fingers returned. The doctor was confident it wouldn't be permanent so I finished the treatment and moved on to thirty-three courses of radiation.

A trip to the doctor every day became my lunchtime routine. This was very exhausting and by the end of the treatments, I was just barely making it through my workday. But God is good, and His grace and strength sustained me through it all.

It has been sixteen months since I was first diagnosed, and I just finished the last of my chemo treatments. I had my final scans and awaited the results. I know that all is well because my God is faithful. My hair is growing back, not fast enough, but that is my vanity. I am getting stronger every day.

From the very beginning, as I began to fight this awful disease, I kept saying, "I will do all it takes to keep it from coming back. *I want to live.*" There were times when I felt like I couldn't take anymore, but *I wanted to live.* There were times when my heart was filled with fear, but *I wanted to live.* Now as I regain my strength, *I want to live* and spend time with my family. *I want to live* and strengthen my relationship with my husband, my best friend. *I want to live* to the glory of God.

> *"I do not think that there is any other quality so essential to success of any kind as the quality of perseverance. It overcomes almost everything, even nature."*
> --John D. Rockefeller

Constant Grace

Carianne

My name is Carianne, and this is my story.

I consider myself an optimistic person, one who always hopes for the better, gives people the benefit of the doubt, and is always thankful for each day I get to exist on this great planet. Life hasn't always handed me roses without the thorns, but with my faith and outlook on life, I've managed to find the beauty even among the thorns.

When my husband and I married in 2005, we had hopes to one day have a house full of children. In 2009, we were blessed with the birth of our first princess, and she changed our world. When she was almost two, we decided it was time to add a sibling to her world and when the test came back positive, we were elated and couldn't wait to share the news! We were excited to catch a glimpse of the little peanut during my ten-week checkup. We did just that. We caught a glimpse of his or her short life. There was no movement, no heartbeat and for a moment, the heartbeat in my own chest stopped. My husband and I left that doctor's office devastated. We never thought we would hear bad news. I suppose we thought we were untouchable because we were young and healthy. After taking time to grieve and waiting to ensure we were good to try again, we did.

In 2012, another princess entered our world. She was beautiful, perfect and brought even more joy into our lives. Again, time went by and we were ready to add a third sibling. Early in 2014, we had a positive pregnancy test. However, after seven short weeks, we lost our baby. Fear filled my mind about what I'd done wrong. Was there something I could have done to prevent yet another loss?

In April 2014, we got another positive pregnancy test and though we were excited, it made us anxious. I was scared to get my hopes up only to lose another baby. I took extra good care of myself and was glad to deal with another round of morning sickness because that is usually a good sign! At my eight-week checkup, I saw our treasured bundle and heard a strong heartbeat. You bet I cried! I started allowing myself to accept the joy of another baby and was hopeful about its future. With this technically being my fifth pregnancy, it didn't take long before I had a belly bump. I couldn't hold it in anymore, literally, so we made a baby announcement stating, "We interrupt November's hunting season to bring you baby #3." My husband appreciated the clever announcement as we wore camouflage and held our bows for the picture; that was right up his alley.

The excitement and support we received was wonderful and just the reactions we were hoping for! At about the fourteen-week checkup, we heard a strong heartbeat yet again. This relieved my anxiety, especially when my baby kicked the heart monitor. I had another active baby in that tight space!

My husband and I were loyal volunteers at one of Ohio's youth camps, and the week-long summer camp with the Ohio

Youth Ministry Network was approaching. We had the choice to have a gender-reveal ultrasound before camp or when we got back. We opted for before so we could share the exciting news with our friends. On a beautiful Friday morning, we took our two princesses and headed to the doctor's office to share in the joyful moment together. Little did we know our visit was going to be far from joyous.

As I lay on the bed and the nurse put the cold jelly on my belly, I said another little prayer, "Be with us, God." Our baby was right there on the screen. Her foot was the first thing we could see clearly. Her little skeleton was adorable, with her fingers, her spine, her legs and arms. But one thing was missing, one thing I was anxious to hear again: her heartbeat. The nurse paused, "I'm afraid I don't have good news for you."

"No!" was all I could muster. Not again! Not me! Why me? I had finally accepted the excitement of a new baby. The timing of her arrival would have been perfect, and we were dreaming of life as a family of five.

How could this be happening?

The forty-eight hours that followed were sleep deprived, steeped in prayer, and some of the darkest hours my husband and I have ever gone through. I had no idea what to expect in the delivery of my eighteen-week-old baby. I figured it had to be a little easier on the body physically, though emotionally it would wipe me out. I was dead wrong.

I physically went through some of the worst pain I have ever experienced. At one point I told my husband I wasn't going to make it, but he had the strength to keep me going. The nurses made me their priority and were at my side throughout the day. They even let their guard down to share in the emotions of the day with us. I had strong contractions that were a minute apart and during that minute-long break, I was throwing up or nearly passing out. With the help of an epidural, my body finally relaxed. Things seemed to settle down enough that my husband took a quick walk to catch his breath and make a phone call to update our family. But upon receiving my text, my husband came rushing back into the room to meet our daughter. Another princess for our family.

As I looked upon her for the first time, a peace washed over me that I didn't expect. Her beautiful hands and feet, her head and face, all the details were there. At eighteen weeks her fingers had nails, the tiny bones that once helped her kick the heart monitor were all there. She was beautiful. We held her, loved her, and gave her what we felt was a very appropriate name, Grace Constance. For us, her name was a reminder that in the midst of life, in the midst of whatever comes our way, God's grace is always constant. In this season and throughout the course of my life, I can definitely say this is true.

During those special hours of holding our daughter, I saw a side of my husband I hadn't seen before. My husband does not cry. After being together for ten years, there was only one time I had seen him shed a tear, and that was at his grandfather's funeral. Yet, in the hospital room, as we held our Grace, my husband shed many tears. I didn't think of him as a weaker man; instead it made my love for him grow stronger. I saw my manly husband weep as he held his precious daughter, knowing these few hours were the only ones we would ever have with her.

My husband and I grew stronger in our marriage and in our love for one another during those dark hours. We held each other, shared in moments of agony and fear, and even found time to laugh. We saw a compassionate and loving side of our young daughters that we had never seen before. We pulled together as a family to help each other walk through that dark valley.

Too often we think we are untouchable. We think bad stuff can never happen to us. However, no one can escape the raindrops, gray skies, and quakes that shake our world. Unfortunately, we don't live in a world of lollipops, unicorns, and rainbows, but we aren't without hope. Hope for another day. Hope that everything has a reason and that there is a season for everything. We keep on living because we choose to do so. Every morning we choose our attitudes toward the day and toward life. I choose joy, love, peace, and hope. A hope that one day I will see my entire family together in a place that is too beautiful for the human mind to comprehend. A place where we don't wear gold around our necks, but we walk on it. A place where pearls welcome us at the front gates and our Creator is the source of light. I have this hope, as an anchor to my soul, that one day we will be together and it will be worth it all.

Though Grace's time on earth was short, her impact was great. I am honored and thankful that others can gain strength and encouragement from our story. We didn't go through this for it to be forgotten or ignored, nor did we go through this to bring permanent gray skies to our lives or to lose our joy of living. We have this story to share, encourage, strengthen, and give hope to others. Maybe others will experience God's constant grace and have hope as well.

> *"Perseverance, secret of all triumphs."*
> --Victor Hugo

Staying Strong

Lucy

My name is Lucy, and I have been bullied practically my whole life. It is one of the worst things for a person to have to go through. It makes you feel scared, alone and depressed. I suffer from depression and anxiety. I was bullied in both junior high and high school, but mostly in high school. I have a few friends who I see every now and again, and they are amazing. They always know how to cheer me up when I'm sad. I see them a lot more now than I did before, which is great. I used to be alone and have no one who would listen to me, but now I'm not.

It all started when I joined seventh grade. I was scared and nervous about moving to a new school, especially since only a couple of girls that I knew well were moving to the same school. I told myself I'd be okay. I caught the bus the first morning and went to my classroom with a friend. At first, I loved it there. It seemed like a nice school, and everyone seemed really friendly. The teacher was nice and said I was very "smiley" and "delightful."

I was starting to make some friends, but my other friend (the one I knew from junior school) seemed to be making more than me. I felt a bit left out. There were a few people in my class who I got along with, but after a while, my friend moved on to her new group of friends and, in a way, left me behind. I was alone, and my friend was ignoring me. After a while, our teacher became ill and left our school. This upset me because she was so nice and the new one wasn't very good.

I soon decided to move into another class where I could make new friends and, I hoped, get a better teacher. I was so happy when I found out that I could move. There was a girl in that class whom I'd already made friends with and we used to go to each other's houses. I thought the move had been a good decision, but it wasn't.

On Monday, the first day I started the new class, I was looking for the classroom. I walked through the corridor and there were people from my new class outside the door, whispering and nudging each other. I walked in and everyone started shouting at me and telling me to go away. I felt so upset, I wanted to hide, go home and go back to my old class. During lessons, the other students were mean. If I had to sit next to someone, they would call me names and treat me like I was diseased and like they didn't want to sit next to me. It was the worst feeling ever. I regretted moving classes so much and blamed myself a lot. I wanted to hide away and never come out. I felt useless, worthless and got very suicidal after a while. I was no longer "smiley" or "delightful" like I once had been; instead, I was being bullied, which made me feel scared and lost. The teacher asked if I was okay. I said I was, but really, I wasn't.

People would leave me out, call me names, throw things at me, make fun of me, trip me in corridors, gang up on me, and hit and poke me. Eventually, I had absolutely no friends at school. It was horrible, and they did it for no reason. They thought it was funny, but they made me believe everything they said, and I felt like I wasn't me anymore. I was called fat, ugly, worthless, loser, loner, four eyes, etc. People used to say no one liked me or I had no friends and some even said I belong in a bin or told me to kill myself and that I was better off dead. They really did make me believe them. It was hard to get through what they were doing and how they treated me. I told myself it was going to be all right, that it would get better. Thanks to my friends, it did get better and people stopped what they were doing. I told people at my school who would really listen to me, and they said it wasn't my fault.

The best thing to do when you're being bullied is to stay strong, keep going, keep smiling and be yourself. It's not your fault that others are doing what they're doing. Remember, you are beautiful and there are other people out there who can help you—you're not alone! No one has the right to make anyone feel bad, so don't let the haters tell you that you're not beautiful. If people are trying to bring you down, it only means you are above them. Stay strong.

"It's not that I'm so smart, it's just that I stay with problems longer."
--Albert Einstein

Earning the Title *Survivor*

Sonya

My name is Sonya—mommy, wifey, sis, boss, nurse, chef, maid, and cancer survivor. Lots of titles, lots of responsibilities, and lots to live up to—and that's just it ... lots to *LIVE* up to, and I *AM* living up to them because I am a SURVIVOR!

Cancer really sucks, ya know that? It is okay to say that, because it's true. It's also true that cancer will change your life in a way that no other event can. I was twenty-nine years old when I was diagnosed. I remember getting the phone call from my doctor on June 19, 2004. *Breast cancer.* The seriousness of her voice and the way she said *those* words were almost more than I could bear. I had myself dead and buried by the time I hung up the phone. I had visions of surgical suites, mastectomy products, a bald head, vomiting, and my three beautiful children and husband looking down on me in my casket. Just in that five-minute conversation, my life fast-forwarded and I went from being a happy wife and mother of three still cleaning up breakfast, planning lunch, and figuring out how to pay for their college, to picking out the color of my casket.

As the days went on, I went so far as to write notes to my kids for those future important days and events I wouldn't be around for. I wrote letters to my daughters for their wedding days. I wrote a letter to my son telling him what type of man Mommy thinks he will be when he grows up and asking if I was right. I even wrote a letter and hid it in the Christmas tree box as I assumed that would be the first year they would put up the tree without me. I told my husband that I would send him a new wife and mother for my kids. I told him he would know that I sent her. He would know because she would be the ugliest woman ever (okay, I may have a tiny bit of a jealous streak), but she would love him and my kids almost as much as I do.

I am all about supporting my family, and my way of supporting them was to act strong at all times, even when I had to fake it. To this day, I believe this whole experience was harder on my family than it was for me. They had to watch helplessly. They had to trust in strangers, my doctors—people who like me but do not *love* me. That is hard. I asked my family to leave me alone the day before surgery because I didn't want them to see me hurting and quite honestly, I didn't know if I could "fake strong" for them and I knew that I didn't want to *have* to.

They came to the surgery anyway, and I did fake strong for them. Now, thinking back, there was one moment that evening before surgery that was life changing. My dad and I were alone, walking around the pond and I was doing my usual "strong daughter" act and said, "It's okay, Dad. Really I am okay with this. I'm just thankful this is not one of my children. The Lord knows I could not handle that, so I am okay with this." My dad looked at me and said, "Yes, but you are *my* daughter, kiddo, and it doesn't matter if you are one, two, or twenty-nine, you're still my child." Whoa. Yes, Dad

... I hear what you're saying. I get it. That's when I looked at him not through the eyes of a daughter but those of a fellow parent. Again, whoa.

I felt a twinge of deep sympathy for this guy whose daughter is sick with the "C" word, followed by a realization that it was ME he was referring to. I immediately felt like I had eaten a hundred cans of spinach and instantaneously put on fifty pounds of muscle. I mean, it was all I could do to not leave him to go find a white sailor's hat and pipe!

I know this sounds horrible, but I would be a liar if I didn't admit it, and a liar I am not. Losing my hair was one of the most dreaded, emotional experiences I've ever endured. I tried so hard to be strong and act like it didn't bother me but my acting skills weren't that good. My poor mom was rubbing my shoulders one morning, as the shots I had to get for my blood counts made me ache everywhere, and she noticed hair just laying on my shoulders, unattached from my head. She gently swept them in her hand

and pushed them aside, hiding them so I wouldn't see. I can't imagine how she felt that day. She's a woman. She gets it. It would be years before she would tell me about that. The pain of what I was about to face hurt her that day. She instinctively tried to protect me by swiping and hiding. I would have done the same thing for my daughter too.

One day, a couple of weeks after my first chemo treatment, as I was coming home from finalizing my trust and durable power of attorney for finance and healthcare (I told you I was preparing to die), I had the window down, and I noticed strands of hair flying around in the car. I ran my finger through my hair and huge chunks of it were between my fingers. Today was the day. My husband was at work, so I called him and bravely stated, "I'm going to have my head shaved today." I was ready. As I neared the wig shop, a place that promised to do this for me in a private, serene room with a beautiful garden oasis visible from the window, I started to hesitate. The closer I got, the more the hesitation turned to panic. I called my friend Bill, who is like a brother to me. He answered, thank God, and when I told him what I was doing he was upset, but he pulled it together and told me to quit being a wimp and get in there and just do it. That tough love and Nike tag line was exactly what I needed. I pulled myself together and walked in. I was strong and confident.

But I was still only acting. I felt weak and vulnerable. I was afraid of what my kids would say. *Will they recognize me? Will I, their own mother, scare them? What will my husband say? He will try too hard to hide his initial reaction to the alien, his wife, standing before him.* Those thoughts leaked in, powerful lil' boogers they are!

Anyway, I walked in, pushing those thoughts aside. A nice lady with a full head of beautiful hair said, "Can I help you?" I quickly and confidently opened my mouth to speak but NOTHING would come out! Those strands of hair I threw out the window took my tongue with them. I just reached up to my hair and pulled out a chunk as the tears filled my lower lids. My eyes burned and I was blinded by the volume before they streamed down my face.

The woman reacted in an empathetic, "Oh, honey, come here." She took my hand and walked me to the room. It was beautiful, just as they had described, from what I could see through my tear-filled eyes. Then the power of her voice, even, calm, and soothing, washed over me as she said, "I cannot and will not do this until your husband is here. You need him." Immediately the waterfall of tears stopped and I could breathe. I agreed. I needed my husband. I needed him to see me bald first. I can't tell you the instantaneous relief she gave me at that moment.

I did go the next day, with my husband, into that same room that seemed even calmer now. I didn't boo-hoo like I had before, but a couple tears did escape—this time privately with my husband holding my hand the entire time. Not much was said, but he reminded me over and over how beautiful he thinks I am, with and without hair. He still tells me that today. I love that man.

Survivors aren't just given that title; they work their butts off for it! They earn it. *I* earned it! I learned through my low times that only *I* can choose to let this defeat me. I had to make that decision both physically and mentally. My doctors can help me through their life-saving treatments; however, I had the bigger challenge of dealing with my mental strength and power. Maybe you've heard someone say that dying from cancer isn't hard—living with it is. Whoever first said that wasn't kidding. However, I am up for the challenge of living with cancer. I have been doing it for a long time, and I will continue to do so until the good Lord says, "Well done, my good and faithful servant."

> *"It does not matter how slowly you go so long as you do not stop."*
> --Confucius

Chronic Fatigue Syndrome Made Me Stronger

Jaaci Carr

Everything happens for a reason. I did not realize this when I was a freshman in high school and was faced with a condition that halted my sports career early. Growing up in a sports-oriented family and being on two varsity teams at that age, I thought my life was ending when I was told I had chronic fatigue syndrome and would not be able to play anymore. The doctors told me to stop all physical activity because it would only worsen the symptoms, which included muscle pain and exhaustion. This was not an acceptable answer for me, and my parents were behind my decision to continue to play volleyball and basketball.

I pushed on and went through many treatments to try to decrease the pain and increase my energy. I felt like a guinea pig, trying any new fad to feel better. I tried B-12 shots, chiropractic adjustments, massages, energy drinks, natural remedies, drops, reflexology, iridology, magnets, a new diet, vitamins, herbs, essential oils, physical therapy, stretching, and much more. I arrived late to school after game nights so I could sleep in. I missed twenty-three days of school that first year I lived with chronic fatigue syndrome. This took a toll on my grades and as a perfectionist, I found that hard.

I would not give up on trying to find a cure, even though the doctors all told me rest was the only treatment for chronic fatigue. Even with rest, they said I would not feel fully refreshed, and to make matters worse, my immune system would be weaker. I would get sick easier and the sickness would last longer than it did for normal people. I would have to deal with this for the rest of my life. Chronic fatigue syndrome never goes away; it may go into remission, but eventually it always relapses.

I went to specialist after specialist; we traveled to the Cleveland Clinic, Fort Wayne, and Toledo. All had different results. Cleveland Clinic told me they could do nothing for me. Fort Wayne said there was no quick fix, and instead they wanted me to cope with my disease, so they prescribed antidepressants and a psychiatrist. This made me feel worse. Toledo told me there was a Fibro and Fatigue Center in Detroit and referred me there.

I went there for months and had multiple blood tests to see what my body was lacking. I then received IVs to help get me back on track. I sat in the La-Z-Boy and received my treatments. The only problems were that I had a two-hour drive there and back, which made me sore and more tired, plus my parents spent loads of money on the treatments that insurance did not cover. I could not continue down this road when I was not seeing results.

I felt like a lab rat at this point and was frustrated over all of the failed attempts, so I decided the best decision for my health was to quit playing sports. I couldn't keep crying after every game and practice; sports were not worth the pain. I chose to finally listen to the doctors, which was a difficult decision for a sixteen-year-old girl. Would I keep my friends? What would I do with my time? Would my college decision change? Looking back, I wish I'd listened to the doctors right away. After I quit playing sports, I felt a little better but struggled with my place in the world.

I wanted to go to college to play basketball and major in early childhood education. Both of those paths changed. Since I would not be able to play sports in college, I decided to start coaching right out of high school. This was a blessing in disguise. I enjoyed coaching and was pretty good at it too. I was able to spread my knowledge and love for the game to young girls, which was gratifying. With the help of my mom and an influential yearbook teacher, I also decided to change my major to integrated language arts. With chronic fatigue I could not have chased after those youngsters all day; high school kids would be more manageable when I was having what I call a "bad day."

What is a bad day in my world? It is a day filled with leg pain that feels like a bruise. Whenever anything touches them, I cringe with pain. Sometimes it feels like someone is constantly punching me. A bad day is taking a shower and being so worn out afterward that I cannot even get dressed. I get to a point where I have to miss work in order to rest and get back to my "normal" feeling, which is below average. I know when I need to slow down, however, and I have developed a high pain tolerance both physically and mentally. On the outside, I look fine so people do not understand my disease. My pain is masked so people tend to dismiss it, or worse, not believe me.

I was bitter for a long time because most diseases have cures, but mine doesn't. I had to make sacrifices, such as not going to help with Katrina cleanup when I was in college because my immune system would be too susceptible to the mold. I even had a hard time going to watch football games in high school because the student section stood the whole game, a move I would pay for the next day. I went through the "Why me?" phase for a long time. I wanted to be normal, but chronic fatigue syndrome did not stop me. One day I came to the realization that God chose me for a reason.

I believe I was chosen because I am strong enough to handle chronic fatigue syndrome. Do I have days where I feel sorry for myself? Yes. I would not be human if I didn't, but now I tend to look at the positives more than the negatives. I was the one handpicked to spread my story of perseverance to people. I am actually one of the lucky ones because many chronic fatigue sufferers go on disability and can't work; some can't have children. I am fortunate enough to have a teaching career I love and a daughter I love even more. I have a full plate of coaching, getting my master's, being the yearbook advisor, and much more.

Through all of these tasks, I have learned to deal with my daily pain and exhaustion, and I am no longer chasing a cure. I am simply living life to the fullest and have overcome this obstacle. I can only hope others who are suffering learn this lesson a little sooner than I did.

My disease is not a death sentence. I can't live a "normal" life because I am special, different, or unique. God chose me, and my chronic fatigue syndrome has made me the person I am today. I was not nearly as sympathetic until I was diagnosed and lived with my illness. Now, I feel for people who experience hardships because I know what they are going through. It has led me in a different direction to new opportunities and even new friends.

One of the reasons I married my husband was because he is one of the few people who understood my disease and helped me through my tough times. I thank God every day for giving me this caring man. He knows I cannot get up at night with our daughter because it would take too much out of me. Do I miss those snuggle times? Yes, but I hope I am showing my daughter that she can achieve anything she sets her mind to, even when she is dealt a difficult hand. I may not be able to get up with her at night, but I am able to work and cope with my disease, which is hopefully going to be meaningful to her when she grows up.

Not only have I found meaning in life, but I have found appreciation too. My disease has made me appreciate family more than I would have if I were healthy. They have supported me along the way through all of my tough decisions. Chronic fatigue syndrome brought us closer, which made me realize that God works in mysterious ways. I have more faith in Him now than I ever did before because after the rain, everything became so clear to me.

Chronic fatigue syndrome has made me stronger and better as a person. I could have dwelled on my misfortunes, but instead I have persevered and am confident I will continue to persevere with the help of my support system. I live by the quote, "You can't stop the waves, but you can learn to surf." I feel as though I am surfing every day of my life.

"Let me tell you the secret that has led to my goal. My strength lies solely in my tenacity."
--Louis Pasteur

My Journey to Discovering My True Self

Lisa Kelly

Do you ever find yourself hurting so much that you don't know what to do with yourself? I have felt this way one too many times throughout my life. This pain made me long for change.

It started when I was twelve years old; my very first boyfriend hit me and left bruises. He was angry all the time, and I was his punching bag. I began to starve myself to change the way I looked, which, in turn, gave me a false confidence. This drastic weight loss and attitude adjustment created a euphoric sense of newness within me, and I forgot about the pain. I covered up the bruises and mustered the courage to walk away from this angry, very damaged boy.

I continued my search to fill the void in my heart. At the age of sixteen, I was raped twice within five months. The first time was on a Valentine's Day lunch date.

After this I began to drink alcohol to escape my emotional and physical pain. The second time I was raped happened when I passed out at a party and my boyfriend and his friends took turns having sex with me. I was devastated, so I decided to change the way I looked. I cut my hair short and changed the color; I even changed the way I dressed. I changed my group of friends so I didn't get too close to anyone.

I needed to change because I thought I could hide my pain, hide who I had become. Being a victim of rape changed me and I didn't want anyone to see that broken side of me, so I molded myself into this new person. This was the only way I could have any version of normalcy. I also wanted to feel safe, so I started dating mean guys who loved to party, do drugs, and fight. I thought that these guys would keep me safe, but instead this just put me in the company of dangerous people. I endured verbal and physical abuse, which led me to drink more to numb the pain and escape the black hole of insanity and chaos.

Even though I was abused, and lost, I had a small glimmer of hope that my life would get better. I knew that one day I would find someone to love me more than I loved myself. I didn't know it then, but that small voice of hope that I desperately clung to was God. This hope gave me the strength to keep putting one foot in front of the other to reach that promised brighter and better tomorrow.

At nineteen, I thought I found that ideal tomorrow when my family and I moved 3000 miles across the country to California. This big move and much-needed change of scenery supercharged me. My opportunity for a new life and better tomorrow had finally come. I got to flee from my past and escape the constant memory of the pain I had endured. I put away the version of myself who tried to drink away the pain. I got to be a new "me." I played the part of a fun-loving girl from the south who was fearless and loved life.

Unfortunately, the move was not a cure for my shattered heart and empty soul. I ended up doing what I knew best: drowning my pain with alcohol and blinding everyone with false evidence that appeared real. They didn't know that I was a fake and that the struggle to find happiness was consuming me. I changed who I was for each guy I dated so I could meet his definition of an ideal girlfriend. I thought that if I were perfect, I wouldn't get hurt or abused ever again. I changed so much that I forgot who I was. I ignored those tiny whispers of hope in my heart and drowned them with more alcohol.

With a lot of partying comes clouded judgment and bad choices. When I was twenty-five, I was raped again on a first date. This time I stared evil in the eyes, and I will never forget the chill that ran down my spine. This rape changed me in a different way than the others. It left me desperate and hurt. A lifestyle of chaos and carelessness had left me vulnerable and unsafe. This rape broke me but it led me to turn to that tiny glimmer of hope that I had been ignoring. I held onto that hope with all my heart and soul and began searching for my true self, the true identity that was buried deep beneath the pain, isolation, and chaos.

God stepped into my life and reintroduced Himself to me in my late twenties. In the midst of my hazy wandering, God brought me an angel. This angel was in the form of a handsome man with piercing green eyes and a voice that could melt your heart with just a simple hello. God used him to show me a new way of living, one filled with true love. I am not just referring to meeting the love of my life but the true, unconditional love of my heavenly Father. Steve and God began leading me hand-in-hand on a healing journey to find my true self.

First, I had to tell my family what had happened to me when I was a teenager. They never knew because I kept all of the abuse a secret. To my surprise, they didn't judge me but embraced and loved me. After I finally told them, I felt a little lighter. My secret lost its power over me. My next step was to trust that God had me in the palm of His hand. God promised to catch me whenever I fell;

He would pick me back up and help me along this journey. I was blessed that God gave me a loving man to stand by my side to encourage me and love me when I couldn't love myself.

The next step to discovering my true self was to let go. I had to let go of control and this image of who I thought I was. I had to break down the wall surrounding me and let in God. I had to strip off lies and clothing and see the raw, naked truth. There it was on the floor: my hat of shame, boots of regret, pants of self-loathing, and the shirt carrying the big, bright, bold label, HOPELESS VICTIM.

Letting go of all of that brought true surrender. I stared back at the truth and began to let it in. God's truth of who I am is a strong, confident, courageous woman who is worthy of love. I AM A SURVIVOR. When I finally surrendered all of the pain and despair, the healing began. During my healing journey, my relationship with Steve grew stronger and we got married.

My healing journey hasn't ended. There are obstacles still to overcome but every day, God reveals more of my true identity to me. If you were to ask me today, "Who are you?" I would tell you that I am a survivor and a confident woman who knows God. I am a wife, a daughter, a sister, and a friend. I am a person who craves growth instead of change. I am the daughter of a heavenly Father who offered me a new life, one filled with unconditional love, healing, and hope for a beautiful future.

You can visit Lisa on her website,
www.breakingmysilence4healing.blogspot.com.

> *"Success is the sum of small efforts,*
> *repeated day in and day out."*
> --Robert Collier

Daughter, Sister, Granddaughter, Best Friend

Erin Attard

Her name was Melissa McGillicuddy-Attard.
She was a daughter, sister, granddaughter,
best friend and surrogate mother to all strays.

She won awards in high school.
She loved music, cupcakes, sparkles,
Christmas and all things pretty.

She was caring and compassionate and loved
her family.

She loved to laugh, party and plan get-
togethers.
She supported and loved her friends
unconditionally.

She loved the underdogs and was especially
kind to all people with special needs. She
made peanut butter sandwiches and gave
them to the homeless.

She had dark days and medical struggles.
She had songs and poetry written about her.
She loved perfume and bubble baths.
She had an eating disorder.
She gave the best hugs.

She was on long, unacceptable waiting lists
to try to get help.

She loved stiletto heels.
She was pretty and had the most beautiful
eyes.
She had a wicked sense of humor and an evil
laugh.

She struggled with anxiety, seizures and
chronic pain.

She loved dragonflies, nature, bunnies and
ferrets.

She was my daughter and best friend.
She lost her life to suicide on September 21,
2011. She was twenty-nine years old.

My daughter's death does not define who she was, what she accomplished or how much she was loved!

My daughter's death blew apart my life. It had such a huge ripple effect on the community, within the family and with our friends. The pain and confusion was unbelievable. Did I not love her enough? Could I have done more? Should-haves and could-haves overwhelmed me. Why would some people not speak her name or talk about her death? Why, when people would see me in the grocery store, did they turn down another aisle so they wouldn't have to speak to me? What were they afraid of?

My child died, and I want people to speak her name, tell her stories, show me pictures, hug and support my family. Would we not do this with any other death?

I started my journey through grief looking for answers, for something to make this rawness go away. I found support groups but not for suicide survivors. My husband and I met many lovely and kind people who had lost children, spouses and friends. These individuals have been our companions through our darkest days, but even these folks really did not get it. Why is there so little support for survivors of suicide?

I shared my story and people in the community eventually started to contact me to share their own stories. I had no idea how many people had been affected by suicide in my rural town; it seemed to be an epidemic!

Seeing a huge need, the bereavement co-coordinator of our local hospice center was very supportive of setting up a survivors' group to allow for a safe and supportive environment for folks to continue talking and sharing. I am very honored to be a co-facilitator of this. We have to keep talking, reaching out and sharing our stories!

I am still appalled with wait times in our medical system, lack of mental health funding and facilities and the lack of education in the school system. I have since gotten involved with our local high school, providing one-on-one bereavement support to teens who are struggling. No one has to make this journey alone.

I am not the same person I was two years ago. In some ways, my daughter's death has made me a better person. I volunteer my time. I have discovered I am a good listener; I am patient and I do not pass judgment on people's lives. People trust me with their most intimate secrets and I seem to bring them some peace by listening. I am kinder to myself and know it is okay if I have a bad day or cry and look at pictures instead of cleaning the bathroom. I have a much greater appreciation of nature. Flowers, birds, animals and sunsets all seem so much more beautiful now, and I find the time to enjoy them. I love to walk my dogs and laugh at their antics. I have learned to forgive people who say things that are not appropriate because I understand they do not get it. I enjoy the small things in life, collecting dragonflies and angels, and I enjoy time with my son.

We have built a beautiful memorial garden for my daughter. I spend hours sitting in this beautiful, meaningful space. We have summer bashes for her friends, and I bake tons of cupcakes with sprinkles for parties. I am invited and go to showers and weddings and enjoy babies named in her honor.

One day at a time, one step at a time, one holiday at a time. Time does not make it easier, but it does change things. My family has started new traditions and we celebrate things in new ways. We will never be whole again but we must keep finding ways to celebrate and things to smile about—my daughter would've wanted it this way.

I have no magic potion to ease my pain, and I am not superhuman. I have surrounded myself with caring individuals who listen to me, hold my hand through my struggles and tell me I am not going crazy. I am just a mom who has lost a child. It is my new life goal to see that my beautiful girl will never be forgotten and perhaps along the way, I can help support another.

"Perseverance is not a long race; it is many short races one after the other."
--Walter Elliot

A Wolf in Sheep's Clothing

JoAnn Buttaro

My name is JoAnn Buttaro, and I am a date rape survivor who has successfully completed counseling after being diagnosed with post-traumatic stress disorder (PTSD). I have seen my attacker through two trials resulting in convictions for sexual assault and rape.

I met him on Match.com in March 2004. We got together for drinks and subsequently returned to his apartment where he drugged and raped me. Because of the high dosage of drugs he put in my drink, I had no memory of the rape but woke the next morning in his bed, naked, sick, knowing I didn't consent. I rationalized that I'd had too much to drink, which resulted in a memory lapse, and I decided to put the incident behind me and move on with my life. But then, I received a call in December 2005 from the Philadelphia District Attorney's office asking if I knew of and had met Jeffrey Marsalis. After confirming that I had, they proceeded to tell me about their criminal investigation of him and how they were led to me.

Marsalis had been arrested for sexually assaulting three women in Philadelphia and while awaiting a 2006 trial, he moved to Idaho while out on bail. In Idaho he raped another woman and was then arrested, which resulted in a search of his apartment where the police obtained a homemade substance he used as a date rape drug. The police also went through his computer and found numerous Match.com profiles, including mine. During the conversation with the assistant DA, like a tidal wave, the memory of our date came flooding back all at once. The events of that evening and the following morning all began to make sense, including the fact I had been unconscious for more than eight hours from only three drinks and was so violently ill for two days later. I relayed all those details to the ADA, and then I was asked if I would be willing to give a statement to a Special Victims Unit detective. I agreed.

Three days later I found myself doing just that, spending about two hours describing my evening and morning with Marsalis. The detective was compassionate as he listened to me explain such embarrassing details. He explained the scale of the investigation into Marsalis (there were dozens of victims), describing to me a man who'd fabricated all aspects of his life except his name. He told women he was an emergency room doctor (the story fed to me), an astronaut in training or a CIA agent, none of which were true. At that moment I knew I would press charges and dedicate myself to putting this violent man behind bars for as long as possible. If I had anything do with it, he would never hurt another woman or see the light of day again!

Although Marsalis was acquitted in the January sexual assault trial, because of my statement to the police he was rearrested in the courtroom for sexual assault and other related charges, and taken back to jail. I mentally prepared myself for the preliminary hearing scheduled later that year but in my wildest dreams couldn't have imagined what was ahead of me. The morning of the hearing, I turned on the news to see his mug shot staring back at me, and a reporter explaining the case against him. I had a good cry and then gathered myself and headed to court.

Sitting and standing in the hallway outside the courtroom were the other victims, attorneys from the DA's office, detectives and FBI investigators, news reporters, and someone who would eventually become one of the most important people to my mental health, a court advocate from WOAR (Women Organized Against Rape). She spoke to me about the counseling services available, although at the time I didn't know how much I was going to need them.

That day I walked into the courtroom, sat on the stand, looked straight at my attacker, and accused him in open court of sexually assaulting me. I was able to gain strength as I answered the questions asked by the ADA about the evening I spent with Marsalis. I also answered questions from his defense attorney and the judge. The longer I sat there and told my story, the more confident I felt that I was doing the right thing.

In the months that followed, I began feeling anxious and just not myself. I remembered the services offered to me by Kathy from WOAR, pulled out the business card, and made a lifesaving phone call to schedule an appointment to meet with one of their counselors. The counselor I met with, Laura, ultimately diagnosed me with PTSD. Through the next several years of regular appointments, she helped me navigate the range of emotions and trauma that would come with being actively involved in the two trials against Jeffrey Marsalis. Because the WOAR counselors and staff only treat victims of sexual assault and domestic violence, they have intimate knowledge of the specific mental health treatment necessary, as well as what to expect and how to manage the seemingly endless court process. Using talk and written therapy, Laura helped me through the worst years of my life. She knows that I am who and where I am today because of her support.

During the first trial in June 2007, I supported the other victims by attending the closing arguments and sitting with them as a united front in the courtroom. We then gathered again to attend the sentencing hearing to listen to the judge call Marsalis, "A wolf in sheep's clothing" and sentence him to twenty-one years in prison and classify him as a sex offender. I felt comfortable and safe with these women because they were the only ones who knew what it felt like to be drugged and raped by this monster. They had also committed themselves the way I had to putting him behind bars for as long as possible.

I continued my therapy sessions with Laura and mentally prepared for the trial in Idaho, where that jury ultimately convicted him of rape. The Idaho Department of Corrections requested that any of his other victims, if they were willing, submit a victim's impact statement to be reviewed by the judge while considering the sentence. In June 2009, the judge sentenced him to life in prison with no parole to be served after the Pennsylvania sentence. Everything I had been working toward for almost four years had finally been achieved. My attacker would never see the light of day again; most importantly, he would never hurt another woman.

At the same time Laura informed me that my counseling would no longer be necessary, as I had progressed to a healthy, healed woman. WOAR was holding their *Take Back the Night* event and because Laura thought I was ready, she asked if I would speak to the group about my experience. I wrote my speech with some guidance from her and presented it while holding on to Laura as tight as I could, although it felt good to say it all aloud. Just as I knew I wanted to pursue the prosecution of Marsalis, now that it was over I knew I wanted to pursue speaking out to others about my attack in hopes of helping other victims or even possibly preventing this from happening to other women. In my mind, I felt it was time to pay it forward. I wanted to give to someone else the same kindness and compassion I had received from so many.

I began by speaking to students at my alma mater, Stockton College, for their yearly *Take Back the Night* event. I spoke to Victims Advocacy Training at WOAR and other crisis centers in South Jersey, which led me to a University of Pennsylvania Victimology course speech each semester. Since moving to Los Angeles in October 2013, I now pursue this full time and have been accepted to the RAINN Speakers Bureau, Strength United of Northridge, UC Irvine Speakers Bureau, and have spoken to several universities in LA County. I have been interviewed for an ABC News "20/20" special and an Investigation Discovery Channel documentary.

When I made that promise and declaration to myself in December 2005, I had no idea what I was getting into or how hard it would be, but I always knew that I made the right decision. I not only saw it to the end but have continued beyond. It's been ten years since a violent predator chose me to be his victim, but now I am in control. Although cliché, time does heal all wounds and you can turn a bad experience into something good.

"Most of the important things in the world have been accomplished by people who have kept on trying when there seemed to be no help at all."
--Dale Carnegie

My Melanoma Story:
Three Diagnoses in One Year

Jennifer Dufresne

Tanning. Tanning was an addiction for me. I tanned in the summer and since I lived in upstate New York, I wanted to keep a little "glow" in the winter. I got that glow from tanning beds. It was basically a yearlong endeavor. It became normal to me.

I was diagnosed with melanoma when I was forty. I started tanning when I was seventeen. In my late twenties and thirties, I did quit using tanning beds and slowed down a lot outside in the summer, but I still always had a tan. I also have other risk factors for melanoma, like multiple moles and multiple atypical moles, but according to my doctors, my melanoma showed its face due to my long-term UV exposure.

March 2012: Round One

It all started when I made an appointment with a plastic surgeon in March

2012 for what my primary physician and I thought was a keloid scar from a minor burn on my right upper arm. I went in thinking I was going to pay a fortune to have it removed, but I just couldn't stand to look at it anymore, especially since the steroid my doctor injected to shrink it had changed its color.

As soon as the plastic surgeon saw it, he knew right away it was not a scar. He examined my lymph nodes and removed the scar with margins to be biopsied. I thought to myself, *what the hell is he checking my lymph nodes for?*

It took about four days for him to call me, but I was already expecting bad news. "Jennifer, it was a melanoma. We need to schedule surgery right away. You need to see another surgeon to perform a sentinel lymph node biopsy, and you need to be scheduled with an oncologist before your surgery." I didn't break down sobbing. I just felt like I was living outside of my body.

Everything was done the same week of my diagnosis. Full body CAT scans, sentinel lymph node biopsy, and wide excision with skin grafting from my abdomen since the melanoma was so large. The recovery was VERY painful but I made it through and all CAT scans and lymph nodes were negative for melanoma. Thank God!

I was on the road to recovery and scheduled for routine skin checks every three months. After a couple of months, I felt pretty much back to normal, but was obviously obsessing over any little change in a mole or new skin growth. I thought I made it through the rough part; now I wanted to move on.

October 2012: Round Two

Six months later, I found a new lesion on my left arm, exactly in the same location as the one on my right arm. It was not from a preexisting mole and it was not brown or black. It looked like a red pimple and was growing and appeared raised. I scheduled a stat appointment with my dermatologist and she thought it was just a picker's nodule (to this day, I have no idea what that is). She wanted to prescribe a cream for it. She said it did not need to be removed.

Well, needless to say, my nasty side had to come out, and I demanded that she remove the lesion or I would find another physician who would. She insisted it was unnecessary and reluctantly removed it.

Five days later, the call came. She said, "I am shocked, Jennifer. It was a melanoma, very aggressive with a high mitotic rate." She is no longer my dermatologist! I immediately called my plastic surgeon. He scheduled my wide local excision immediately, along with sentinel lymph node biopsy by another surgeon and another round of CAT scans. Here we go again!

The surgery went well. No skin graft was needed, and CAT scans revealed that my lymph nodes were clear of melanoma. I'd dodged another bullet! I was referred to a dermatologist in NYC who is affiliated with Sloan-Kettering and started back with three-month checkups.

March 2013: Round Three

One year after my first diagnosis and six months after my second, my hair stylist saw a mole on my scalp that had not been there previously. She told me to let my oncologist and dermatologist know just so they could keep an eye on it. I had my oncologist take a look, and he wanted it removed to be on the safe side because it was almost black. My plastic surgeon removed it in his office and the call came a few days later that it was again, another melanoma.

This time, I freaked out! I didn't know what the hell was going on with me. I was doing everything I was supposed to be doing. I started taking supplements, was totally obsessive about wearing sunscreen and hats, and it happened AGAIN?

Fortunately, it was a very superficial melanoma and my plastic surgeon was able to do the wide local excision without any grafting. The mole was located underneath a bunch of long, dark brown hair and I cannot even find where the scar is. Another blessing!

Today: My New Normal

Since my diagnoses, I have had numerous biopsies and most of my moles have been dysplastic. And while that means abnormal for most, for me, it's my normal.

Life is different now. I advocate as much as I possibly can about the dangers of tanning beds and sun exposure. I tell my story to people in my community. Some of them listen; others pretend to listen but still want that tan. I would like to think that if I were in their shoes, I would listen and stop tanning, but I know how tanning addiction works and I am not sure what I would do.

I do know that when people see my scars, which most of time I have covered up, they feel bad for me. That is NOT what I want. I do not want sympathy from anyone because in reality, I did this to myself. I wanted to tan, and I knew it was not good for me but I did it anyway. I had the "it will not happen to me" mentality, which is what I'm sure most people still feel when I tell my story.

Has life changed for the worse since melanoma? Not a chance. While I wish I didn't have melanoma, I am proud of the person I have become because of it. I cherish every single day I spend with my husband and my family. I appreciate the little things in life that I took for granted before. The things I used to worry about before melanoma do not mean a thing to me now.

I never in my wildest dreams thought I would be strong enough to deal with my diagnosis, but I proved myself wrong. My strength amazes me sometimes and I hope my story will make a difference in someone's life, even if it is just for one person.

Life has changed, but life is good!

" . . . be thou faithful unto death, and I will give thee a crown of life."
--Revelations (2:10)

Life with Autism

Richie Jewell

My name is Richie Jewell. I'm twenty-two years old and have had autism since I was born. Like everyone else in the world, I have an up-down life like a seesaw. I have endured teasing, depression, and a struggle to adapt in places such as schools. I have watched helplessly as my parents divorced and struggled with my disability and its resultant problems, including speech and language, communication, awkwardness in social situations, and an elevated vocal response to frustration.

Despite all these horrible obstacles, I have overcome the problems in my life by using my own set of coping skills:

1. Getting through one day at a time.
2. Knowing that happiness and smiles triumph.

When I had no friends due to the disability, I pretended that my stuffed animals were friends, and I practiced my social skills with them. Whenever I'm in a negative situation, I picture myself in a beautiful, natural scene with happiness all around me. I also remind myself that everything happens for a reason. I always ask myself, "Why do we fall? So we can learn to pick ourselves up." I also write poems from my heart with the help and comfort of family and friends. My hobbies also keep me happy. These include animals, wrestling, movies, writing, and inspiration. All of these seemingly separate things make up the pieces of the huge puzzle of my life.

So you're curious what I do for a living, right? Currently, I work at a local library in Beacon, NY. Outside the job I'm a writer, motivational speaker and world autism advocate. As an advocate, I reach out to people and raise their spirits. I'm writing a book titled, *This Is Me: Life with Autism*, which talks about my lifelong struggles and triumphs with the disability. I do speeches at schools and libraries to raise awareness of autism and world problems and to inspire people to new heights.

Why have I chosen activism? I'm doing this for the people who have been laughed at, ridiculed, and looked at the wrong way, for those who have been told they won't go far in life or who have been bullied. By speaking, I show them that we are in this together. I want to show support to people who are in a struggle like I was. I want to be a symbol that proves anything is possible.

I have a dream that one day this world will rise above the hate and realize what we are doing to ourselves. I hope one day we will treat each other with kindness. This dream will become a reality if we all follow the steps: think, act, and change.

Gandhi once said, "We must become the change we want to see." Believe that you can change the world, act in accordance with the change, and it will happen. My theory is that changing the world cannot be done through force but must be done by educating ourselves. If that happens, then the dream can become a reality and finally my voice will be heard.

You're probably thinking that I'm a dreamer. Through my experience, I know that I'm not alone. The message I want to send is that anyone with a disability can make this positive change happen. Everyone has a voice to be heard.

I learned a long time ago that you don't have to scream and holler to get attention. In fact, I have found that if a person has enough courage to speak softly, people will listen. It's a slow process, but it can be done.

I'm just an average person trying to make a big change in the world so we can live in a healthy, peaceful, beautiful environment. Recently, after celebrating my twenty-second birthday, I took part in a challenge during which I grew a beard for a full year to raise awareness for autism and anti-bullying. It's just one of the many awareness projects I participate in.

We have a long, hard road ahead of us. However, we will never give up. Do not pray for an easy life. Hope for the strength to endure a difficult one. If you're going through a difficult life, just remember: you are not alone. Don't look backward into the past because you will fall. You can't spend your life looking back. You must spend your life looking forward, because you can't change what has happened. If I look back, there's someone else who is looking forward that will go right by me. Your life is your message to the world. Make it inspiring and create a difference!

Accept responsibility for your life. Know that it is you who will get you where you want to go and want to be—no one else. Reach into your heart and soul to discover your talent. Sometimes talents fade away and you lose something special, so hold on to those you have. Follow your dreams and heart by listening to that *whisper* inside your head. If you listen to it, you'll go somewhere. Cherish your visions and dreams because they are the blueprints of your achievements.

Be yourself and be proud of doing so because you are original, special for you who are. If I could snap my fingers and be non-autistic, I would not, because then, I wouldn't be me. Autism is part of who I am and what makes me so unique. Like I said before, everyone has a story to tell, and it is our duty to make the best out of what life has given us. This is who I am and always will be: I am Richie Jewell.

> *"Victory is always possible for the person who refuses to stop fighting."*
> --Napoleon Hill

From Dark Days into the Light

James Siburt

My name is James Siburt, and on October 5, 2005, my life changed. The day began like any other. I was working at a furniture rental company and was sent to a home to pick up merchandise from a customer who'd requested we come by to take away the items he'd rented.

When my partner Eric and I arrived, Eric remained outside to make room in the truck while I went inside and asked the client—who was not past due—why he wanted to return the merchandise. The customer, clearly disturbed, began pacing back and forth in his living room. He explained that while he was paying for a fifty-seven-inch television, the one he had measured only fifty-one inches. He then accused the rental company of messing with his money—although, he used much stronger language than that. He went on to say that no one messes with his money. He then threatened to physically harm both my partner and me.

I looked at the television's model number and found that the customer was right—it was a fifty-one-inch screen. I suggested, then, that he leave everything in place and work it out with the store manager rather than returning the television.

At that moment, Eric, who happened to be friends with the customer, walked in. The customer told Eric to "shut up" and told us to get our stuff out immediately. I felt nervous, both because of the customer's demeanor and because my partner wasn't the type to react well to being spoken to like that.

We each grabbed one end of the large television set and carried it out. While getting it positioned in the back of the truck, I asked my partner about the customer's physical threats—whether he was the type to carry through with them, and if we should just get out of there now.

Eric didn't seem nervous, so we went back in to pick up the rest of the items being returned. The customer was still pacing back and forth and, as we began to move the couch outside, he entered his bedroom and turned his back to us.

His silence was eerie, but I focused on the job at hand. As we were trying to get the couch through the door, Mr. Brown began shooting. At the time, I thought he was shooting toward me—maybe just trying to scare me. Later, at the hospital, I discovered that he aimed all six of those .45-caliber hollow points right at me—and two of them hit their target.

I knew I'd been hit when my right arm suddenly went numb. I dropped my end of the couch and yelled to my partner that I'd been hit. Then I ran for the door, getting hit again.

I made it to the truck, but stayed in front of the house so as not to abandon Eric. I looked toward the window and noticed the cup holder filling with blood. The pain in my ribs distracted me.

When Eric finally came out of the house and saw me, he started freaking out about the amount of blood in the cup holder.

He begged me to get out so he could drive, but my ribs were in so much pain, I couldn't manage the maneuver. Eric jumped on my lap and took the steering wheel while I handled the brakes and gas. We got about two blocks away before we hit a dead end. Eric jumped out of the truck and called 9-1-1. I stayed calm and told him I'd be fine—after all, I was only shot in the shoulder and would return to work the next day ... or so I believed.

After surgery, I found out the true extent of my injuries. The first bullet hit a bundle of nerves in my right shoulder, leaving me paralyzed. The bullet blew my shoulder bone apart and then ricocheted into my ribs, cracking seven of them. It lodged itself between two ribs, where it still sits today. My shoulder bone had to be pieced back together and held with metal mesh, rods, and screws. A second bullet hit the left side of my stomach, traveled through my bowel and out the right side of my back. It was later found in the seat of the truck. When I eventually left the hospital, the hole in my stomach had to be cleaned by my wife or me with peroxide and saline, and packed with gauze.

When I woke in the ICU, my ribs, stomach, and shoulder hurt. After another surgery, I was able to try walking—which brought a pain so intense, it nauseated me. However, I fought it and eventually was released from the hospital.

At home, I still couldn't walk very well. I couldn't use my right arm at all at first and when I eventually regained some use of it, it was so weak, I couldn't even open a jar. And to think not that long ago I'd been going to the gym as well as lifting televisions and couches at work.

An in-home nurse and occupational therapist worked with me and slowly, I began to improve. Still, one year later, the hole in my stomach remains, and after having the metal rods and mesh removed from my shoulder, I still have partial paralysis in my right arm, wrist, and fingers. I've had eight tendons transferred, intense hand therapy, a third stomach surgery with eight inches of bowel removed, and blood clots that developed in my knees and traveled to my lung, requiring a vena cava filter implant.

I've been through hell, and am not quite back—and this is just a condensed version of my story. However, through it all—through the mental issues, the physical limitations, the surgeries, and the pain—I've never given up. Shortly after my experience, I started the Victims Support page on Facebook. We're dedicated to helping all victims of violent crimes find a way through those dark days and back into the light.

Today, you can find James on his Facebook page, Facebook.com/victims.support where he gives emotional support, finds resources and sends care packages to survivors in need.

"There is no failure except in no longer trying."
--Elbert Hubbard

Anna's Story

Anna

My name is Anna, and I grew up in what I consider a bit of a fairy tale. My dad is a self-employed physician, and my mom was a teacher before my little brother and I were born; after, she became a stay-at-home, homeschooling mom. We traveled to exotic places and lived in a beautiful home. The four of us genuinely enjoyed each other's company. We had many loyal and loving friends; we were blessed with good health, a strong faith, and a great God. I was—am—thankful for all of this, and was well aware there are very few children who have a childhood like mine.

I've always had a passion for being a role model, maybe because I looked up to my parents and their hard work, generosity, and kindness, or maybe because when I was a kid there were older kids who I adored but who didn't pay much attention to me. I took this self-assigned role very seriously, but was poignantly aware that I didn't have a story. Although I had experienced the loss of my grandfather and my "adopted" grandma, I hadn't really known much pain. Not much of a testimony to share. How could I speak into the lives of others and radiate joy with conviction when I had never really had a circumstance that would test my own joy? Of course I was happy—I had no reason to be otherwise!

The summer following my eighteenth birthday and high school graduation found me on my knees often, praying for the Lord to use me in an extraordinary way. Looking back, that was a pretty audacious prayer, but even after all that I've been through since, I wouldn't change it. I didn't want to live in a comfort zone my whole life. I wanted to impact others, to have a story, to have a *voice.* Even after praying, fasting, and seeking the Lord, I did not feel led down any specific path, so I simply decided to enroll at a local university, start on my general education, and hope that I would be guided.

In the middle of September, I began to grow tired from simple activities like walking across campus and climbing stairs— really any physical activity, which was not typical for me as an in-shape former dancer. On top of losing energy, I came down with a terrible body-wracking cough. It continued for about five weeks, at which point my mom took me to the pediatrician. I had a chest x-ray, which was clear, as well as a prescription for steroids and other antibiotics.

A week later, however, my health seemed to be deteriorating; I began blacking out, unable to stand without losing consciousness. My parents finally took me to the hospital for a blood draw. About ten minutes after arriving home, our phone rang. It was the hospital, and they wanted us in there immediately. Hemoglobin is a protein in the blood that carries the oxygen from the lungs throughout the body. A low hemoglobin level for a normal person is 11.7. Mine was 3.3. The easiest explanation was a virus. They started blood transfusions, admitted me to the hospital, and we went to bed believing everything was fine. Why wouldn't it be?

The following afternoon I woke from a nap and noticed that neither of my parents were in the room. I wasn't concerned at first, but when five minutes dragged into thirty, I began to worry. Finally, they both returned, and my heart sank. They didn't need to say a word; I could tell from their faces that something was seriously wrong. The doctor filed in behind them, followed by a nurse or two and social workers. Leukemia—cancer— my parents said. A so-called *good* leukemia, as it was treatable with a high survival rate, but still cancer. Naturally, I began sobbing and my first question for the doctor was whether I was going to survive. It was reiterated that the survival rate was high, but they said that they weren't going to lie to me; I could die from this. I still trusted my God— I did—this just was not at all what I had envisioned His plan for my life would look like. When I had asked to be used in an "extraordinary" way, I guess I had meant an extraordinarily good way. An easier way. My idea of a better way. This one, however, would call for a two-and-a-half-year treatment. I knew that He *could* heal me, now I just had to trust He was willing to.

Fear is a scary thing. Yes, that sounds obvious, but bear with me. Fear paralyzes us, restricting us from conquering it. When I allowed frightened thoughts to roam freely in my mind, I often found that I could not fight, in this situation, for my life. Fear has the ability to shut you up and shut you down. The Bible talks about taking every thought captive, and my goodness, is that right! There were two options: fight for all it's worth, pray for victory, and live; or roll over and die, accepting defeat. I chose plan A.

The first month of treatment was brutal, but imperative. This was when they hit my 98 percent cancer-filled bone marrow with the big guns, desperately trying to induce remission. Steroids were the "big guns," 100 mg a day for a month. If anyone has ever been on steroids, they will know the frightening effect they can have on our minds. All too often my thoughts were not my own, demented by one drug or another. There are few things scarier than not knowing what to think, and I found myself in that position quite often. I was fantasizing the worst, because if this month's treatment didn't work, I most likely would not survive.

I still remember getting the call from my oncologist thirty days post diagnosis regarding the bone marrow biopsy, which would tell if treatment had worked, if I was in remission. I was upstairs, and I heard the phone ring and my mom answer it. I was paralyzed. She came up to me and burst into tears. Treatment was working! A few days later, we found out that I was in remission. In February 2014, they tested my bone marrow again, and I was totally cancer-free. Treatment continues through spring of 2016 to ensure this fact remains. It's still terrifying.

I discovered some things while I was venturing through this. Anger is a monster. It grabbed me by the ear and yanked me through the mud of misery until I was so covered in it that I could barely breathe. Bitterness rotted me inside out. When I allowed things like bitterness and anger to breed in me, it was disgusting. I get angry and bitter. I'm human. It wasn't easy. It isn't easy. I get so darn sick of it, and I don't understand hardly any of it. Why did He let this happen? What will happen next? I hate not knowing. But I do know one thing: *He knows*. While I might hate being in the dark (He's not really one to leave our life map out for us to peek at), I know that He knows. It's a trust thing. It's not easy—trust—but I'm pretty sure the Creator of the universe knows what path I'm on. I don't know what the future holds, but I am confident in Who holds my future.

I've never been one to hold back my emotions or thoughts. Suffering has a certain beauty. Pain can cut to the core of a person and reveal every raw bit of him or her. For some, that might be terrifying, but I loved it. It was genuinely painful to "fake" how I was doing and feeling. I answered plenty of times that I was "good," and afterward I would cry my eyes out because it simply wasn't true. I was a wreck. According to the docs, I was doing very well, treatment-wise. In fact, as I write this, I am through all the intense treatment. Although my blood counts took hits at times, they never once had to cut my chemo for my body to function properly. I was so blessed with the physical healing process.

Psychologically, though, I'd been at the end of my rope more times than I would like to admit and was in counseling. I was dealing with questions that most people my age probably don't ask for many more years, if ever. Questions about my beliefs, my purpose here, my God. It cut me to the core, and I certainly bled—tears, burning hot emotions, rage. It was as if I was being broken just to be healed in a different, better way. It was painful, but a kinder, more compassionate, more trustful, more thankful self was emerging. It takes a furnace to create a beautiful piece of pottery.

I remember my mom sharing the age-old adage, "When the going gets tough, the tough get going." Common as it may be, it's true. Perseverance requires support, strength, and bravery. I'm tough, have been since I was a little girl and knocked out my front tooth climbing a pole in my grandpa's basement without shedding a tear. I'm a fighter, ever since my little brother decided I wasn't his boss. I'm a survivor, beating cancer proved that. The going got tough, so I got going. Trials create strong people, but they are weak people until they are through and can look back from where they've come. I was not qualified to beat cancer and to emerge better. God doesn't choose strong people. He chooses weak ones so that through them, others can see His strength.

I will never be as strong as I would like to be. After going through this, I'm certainly stronger than I was, but I'm still weak. I heard so many people saying, "He doesn't give you anything you can't handle." I don't think that's true. I was an unequipped basket case when I first got the news, and many times afterward. He gives us things we can't handle *alone*, but with Him, we can take on the world. He provided such a profound peace and comfort that was certainly not me.

I know myself—control-freak Anna always has to have her ducks in a row before she can be calm about a situation. The peace wasn't me. The strength wasn't me. When I was weak, then I was strong.

Through all this, I have come to believe that trials such as the one I experienced—conditions in which perseverance is required—can have only two effects on the individual. They can make you better, or they can make you bitter. Oftentimes during the situation, bitterness wars with betterness, allowing both sides to ferment. Ultimately, however, only one can emerge as victor. We can choose to become angry and cynical when nothing seems to go our way, when things happen that shouldn't have happened and when we decide that being angry and miserable is better than being happy. We can also choose to see the situation as a learning experience. Not that we don't become angry and miserable at times—I know I have. The difference, however, is that I don't stay that way. I could decide that since life is so fragile, it's not even worth doing anything with because tomorrow isn't promised. In a way, I'd be right. Tomorrow *isn't* promised. My next breath isn't promised, and neither is yours. This one—the one you're breathing just as you read—this one is, and I decided today that to the best of my abilities, I will enjoy each breath.

Even though the Lord's "signature move" is bringing beauty from ashes and light from darkness, and everything is pointing to that being His plan for me, I still get scared. However, I've made a choice. I will not live in fear, petrified that something horrible is about to happen. I will see the beauty in this day—the color of the trees, the laughter of my family and friends—and choose to be kind and accept the joy from my Savior. It's a decision every single day. Will I let bitterness or betterness win today? Will I live to the fullest, or decide it's not worth it? Will I let fear cripple me, or will I choose to say "No way, not today!" when it tries to hold me back?

I don't know about you, but when my days here are done, I want to be able to say that *I lived.*

> *"A leader, once convinced that a particular course of action is the right one, must....be undaunted when the going gets tough."*
> --Ronald Reagan

Baffle that Bully!

Chase Anichini

Hi! I'm Chase. I'm 10 years old and in fifth grade. I want to tell you about my experience with being bullied and what I did about it.

For me, school was great until second grade. None of my close friends from first grade were in my class, which kind of bummed me out, so I was really excited to make friends with a girl in class. We liked each other so much that we spent all of our time together. Then, one day out of the blue, she started being mean to me. She criticized my clothes, rolled her eyes when I talked, made fun of my name, and told me I was stupid. I was so confused! This girl was my friend, and I didn't do anything wrong. I kept thinking, "What happened?" and "Did I do something wrong?" My feelings were very hurt, and I think what happened with her made me kind of sensitive and defensive.

Another day, some boys in my class heard her telling me to stop being so sensitive. That must have made them think it would be fun or easy to pick on me. So then those boys started saying mean things to me. They told me to shut up whenever I talked and said that nobody cared about me and no one wanted to hear about my life. I didn't really want to tell the teacher because I thought that would give them extra attention. So I pretended like I didn't care and tried to ignore them, but they wouldn't leave me alone! During lunch and recess I tried to find my friends from first grade, but this girl and these boys followed me around, constantly pestering and picking on me. So even on the days when I did find my good friends, those bullies were still there in the background trying to ruin my day. Some days I hid in the bathroom so they couldn't find me. I was so sad.

I talked to my parents about it, and they talked to the teacher. My desk was moved away from the bullies and the school agreed not to put the girl (who was the worst bully) and me in the same class in third grade. Then came summer, and it was so wonderful! I had months away from those bullies!

On the first day of third grade, I saw that the boy who was the head bully from second grade was in my class <u>again</u>. He had okay behavior during the first few weeks, but then, like clockwork, it all started again. And just my luck, he got two other boys involved and the three of them began trying to ruin third grade for me. They picked on me constantly, mimicked me, and messed with the things in my desk.

I told the teacher, and she got the principal involved. The boys got in trouble for one day, and then it all started again. I felt like I had nowhere to go and nowhere to hide. I was miserable, and nothing was helping.

What I Did to Make Things Better

That was when I got fed up! I decided I'd had enough and there was no way they were going to win. All along I'd been talking to my parents about how to handle the bullies, but over Christmas break we decided to change things up and created this strategy—these three steps—that I would follow every time one of these kids was mean to me. Basically, it was a combination of

- Maintaining my cool, and
- Doing or saying something that would confuse (baffle!) the bully.

By combining these steps, I hoped to stay calm and happy no matter what they said or did.

I went back to school armed with my new strategy; I decided I'd call it a game, because that would make it seem more like fun. I was actually kind of nervous the first day I tried it, but it worked! Here's what happened: this boy started saying mean things to me and rather than react or try to hide, I did my calming stuff. Then, I said to him kindly, "Hey, you play basketball, don't you? How's the season going?"

I'm telling you, you have never seen a more confused kid! He kind of screwed up his face, scrunched his eyebrows, and started stammering, "What … What… What are you talking about basketball for? I didn't say anything about basketball!" Then he walked off shaking his head.

After that, the next day, I was sort of looking forward to going to school so I could try it again. Day after day, my game continued to work. After a couple of weeks, I was excited to go to school because I felt back in control and like I could handle anything! I made it impossible for the bullies to enjoy picking on me. And guess what happened next? They decided to leave me alone!

One of the most important things about the game is that when I played it, I was not only calm but nice—sincerely nice. That's all part of not sinking to their level and not letting them change me. I thought maybe by treating them with kindness, they might even see that is a better thing to do—well, at least I hoped so!

How I Realized I Wanted to Help Other Kids

I was happy with the situation for a while, but then I noticed my old bullies had started picking on some other kids. I remember coming home one day and saying to my mom, "Those other kids should do what I did to get rid of those bullies."

My mom asked, "Well, would you like to tell them what you did?"

If this had happened today, I would for sure walk up to one of those kids and tell them about my game. But back then, I wasn't ready for that. It was still too recent, you know? So I said, "Not really. But I'd still like to help somehow."

Then, we brainstormed: Should we make a video and put it on YouTube? Should we tell the school what we figured out? Should we write a book about my experiences? How about a book with a cute fictional character? Now you're talking! It seemed easier to share my personal story through a cartoon character than as myself.

My mom and I wrote the first draft together. My sister and I named the characters while we were swinging on the swings in our backyard. Then my sister offered to draw the characters exactly how I described them. I said I would have to be the one who colored them in. That is pretty much it!

To tell the truth, when our book *Baffle That Bully!* first came out, I felt a little funny telling people about it because I didn't want anyone to think I was saying something bad about my school. Also, I didn't want people to be able to figure out who I was talking about. I didn't want to make those kids' lives even more difficult—even though they had been so mean and rude to me. That's not the way to make things better.

Then I realized that the point of my game and the point of the book is overcoming bullying by sticking up for yourself, believing in yourself, and treating everyone with kindness—not ever sinking to their level. So, by telling people about the book, I was telling them about something positive and helpful—I wasn't saying something bad about those bullies. Over time, I have realized it's really not about the bullies at all; it's about me! What matters is how I feel about myself, how I treat others, and how I react to others when they do something I think is mean. Thinking someone is mean is just that: a thought. And my thoughts are something I can control.

The first time I read my book to someone else was when my teacher at my new school invited me to read it to my fourth grade class. It was awesome! The kids in my class were literally on the edge of their seats as I read each chapter—it was very cool! Then everybody sat down and did some of the activities that Scarlett (the main character) asks them to do. Everyone was excited to go out to recess to see if there were any opportunities to try out the game. Some of them came back very excited because they had tried the strategy and it worked! Kids who had been mean to them had literally walked away kind of confused because of what my classmates did. The kids in my class felt in control!

Now, we have a website where we blog and do lots of other helpful things. My mom and I take questions from kids who've read the book and we answer as Scarlett—helping individual kids with their own bully problems. It's called *Ask Scarlett*. My mom has been creating some happy, positive artwork and quotes that can help people feel like they aren't alone.

In October of 2013, my mom and I spoke at a bully conference held by the California School Resource Officers' Association. We shared our story and 3-step strategy for empowering the targets of bullying. Afterward, so many people came up to me and said how proud they were of me. They bought their own copies of *Baffle That Bully!* and I even autographed them. The workshop we gave that day is now one of three workshops available through our website. It feels so good to be able to turn that terrible experience into something so positive!

We are already thinking about other friendship and school kid troubles we'd like to write about. Scarlett and her friends are going to tackle some other topics soon; maybe it will become a series. I also think it would be really cool to have lunchboxes with Scarlett on them saying, "I'm a bully baffler!"

I never want anyone to go through what I went through. I wanted to write the book and share what I learned, because it changed my life and helped me be happy again. If I can get through it, other kids can too!

Chase Anichini is a well-adjusted and happy sixth grader who loves math, history, and reading. In her free time Chase studies voice, acting, ballet, jazz, tap, and gymnastics and pursues her passion for musical theatre. She stays involved with anti-bullying advocacy through her website BaffleThatBully.com and as a member of Theatre of Peace, a group of young professional actors who travel to schools to perform Tunnel of Bullying (part of the Beyond Bullying curriculum created by the non-profit Interactions for Peace). Because of her perseverance and passion for performing arts, Chase landed the lead in two musicals in 2013 and 2014. Recently, she won the Vic Kops Children's Challenge Award.

"Defeat is simply a signal to press onward."
--Helen Keller

Enjoying the View from Life's Rollercoaster

Alexus

My name is Alexus, and I am eighteen years old. When I was three, I lost my mom to a disease called lupus. I have an older brother whose name is Kyle. I lived with my dad and Kyle until I was about three years old. Before my mother's death, my brother and I went to a babysitter who we called Kiki. Kiki was very close with both of my parents and family.

Before my mom passed away, she asked Kiki to do everything in her power to make sure that my brother and I were taken care of. Kiki promised my mom she would take care of us because she loved us and wanted to make sure we grew up in an environment that would give us a bright future. She wanted to watch us grow up and become the best that we could possibly be. Around this time, I started spending the night at Kiki's a lot more than usual. When I stayed there, I liked the way it felt, and I liked how I continued to have a mother figure in my life. Things were tough with my dad, and staying in his house just didn't seem right. After staying with Kiki for a long time, I mentioned that I wanted to live with her. Without hesitation, Kiki said that I was more than welcome.

When I was three years old I decided to permanently live with Kiki. I had lived with my mom and dad up until this time. Everything seemed to fall into place living with Kiki. I had someone who made sure I had everything I needed and way more. I had shelter but most importantly, I had a loving home. A while later, my dad decided times were hard and that I had to come home so that my Social Security money could go toward fulfilling my needs while living at his house. He said he couldn't afford to keep everything, pay my medical bills, and pay for my brother if Kiki got full custody of me. Kiki quickly said it wasn't about the money to raise me and that she would continue to help and raise me the best possible way, even if she didn't have custody of me. Once Kiki said this, we all decided that I would stay and live with her. My dad said he would help out when he could, which wouldn't be often. He signed a paper that stated Kiki could have me treated for anything and take me places, but she wasn't my legal guardian.

I attended an elementary school down the street from my dad's house, and then progressed to middle school. Eventually, it was time to decide which high school to attend. I was supposed to go to the same high school my brother attended. My brother told my dad and Kiki there was no possible way he would allow me to go there. He told Kiki and my dad how terrible that school was and how he hated it. He said there was too much fighting, and he didn't want me around that. He also said the educational focus wasn't where it should be because the kids who go to that school don't care about their futures or what happens to them after graduation.

At the time, I attended Our Lady of Perpetual Help and Parish School of Religion

(PSR), a weekly after-school class in which you learn about the Bible, God and ways of the Catholic Church. The woman in charge of PSR was Mrs. Dusseau. She found out I wanted to attend Central Catholic and told me that she would do everything in her power to help me go there.

Months later, I got a phone call from Mrs. Dusseau saying that many donors had stepped up and were very willing to help me pay for tuition. Years later, I still write these donors cards every holiday and keep them updated about my education and sports. It completely took my breath away that people who had never met me were more than willing to help me attend the school of my dreams.

In the blink of an eye, freshman year came to an end and it was time for sophomore year. My dad still refused to help pay for tuition. Mrs. Dusseau told me not to worry, that we would figure out something. Many of the donors who had donated freshman year initially said they would only be able to help for one year. When sophomore year came around, some of those who said they wouldn't be able to donate again *did* donate. They said I made them feel like part of my family. They loved the fact that I had written them cards and kept them updated with my life and sent them my sport pictures. They loved the fact that I told them all about my education in the cards and what I planned on doing in the next couple of months.

When sophomore year ended, it was time for junior year and still my dad was not willing to help. Many prior donors and new donors came together to help me pay for my tuition. I am now at the end of my junior year; I only have a week left. Tuition is already due for next year. Many donors have stepped up once again to help my dreams come true and allow me to attend an amazing high school.

I thank God every day for allowing me to live this amazing life filled with so many people who have blessed me with amazing opportunities. Many people stay down when life knocks them down, but I've learned that no matter what, life goes on. No matter how many bad things happen to you, you won't ever be able to change it, so why look at life negatively? Life is beautiful, and there are good things out there that you can take and make more of. Looking back at my life and knowing that I lost my mom when I was three years old, it makes me truly realize just how short life really is. So many people take their lives for granted when someone else is out their fighting for theirs.

The one thing that gets me through anything and everything that I am dealing with is Kiki. Without her, nothing in my life could've been accomplished. She is the one and only person who helped me when nobody else could or would. She has been the biggest hero in my life. She has been the only person I can count on 100 percent of the time, no matter what the problem is. My brother has also been a positive influence in my life and never lets me give up on my dreams. Mrs. Dusseau has also made a huge impact in my life, helping me shoot for my goals.

Without God, nothing could have happened. I am glad that I am able to learn so much more about him and my faith every day in my religion class because it has made me so much stronger. I may have been knocked down two or three times, but as long as I stand up four or five, then I'm making progress. I am sure in life there will be many more surprises, but something that always gets me through is thinking about my future.

You must be able to take the past and look at it in the most positive way and remember how much you have learned from that! I thank God every day for the challenges He has put in my life, because without them, there is no possible way I would've become as strong as I am today. I also thank Him each and every day for the positive people He has put in my life. Without them, there is no way I would be where I am today. Life is a rough up-and-down rollercoaster but if you hang on tight and enjoy the view, you will see many sights you never thought you would. Seeing all of this, you can better yourself in so many ways.

"Good luck is another name for tenacity of purpose."
--Ralph Waldo Emerson

Reaching the High Diving Board

Sandy Schussel

When I first began practicing law, I believed I had started a career that would bring me adventure and joy, a career I could be passionate about and would leave me feeling fulfilled. A few years into it, however, I found it to be a career with long, tedious hours, mountains of paperwork, unhappy people everywhere and endless arguing and posturing. I believed I was trapped by the need to support the lifestyle I thought a lawyer was supposed to be living, by the belief that I didn't know what else I wanted to do, and by fear of taking a chance on change.

Sometimes, life has a way of making changes for you regardless of your thoughts and fears. As the excessive '80s ended, I lost my three largest clients in a period of about fourteen months. After that, two things became clear: we had to cut expenses, and I had to give up a career I despised. So we sold our huge old "money pit" of a home in an exclusive neighborhood in northern New Jersey and found a new home in a pleasant community near Princeton. We cut our expenses significantly but added two hours of commuting to my already ridiculously long days.

On the morning of December 31, 1991, I was driving my wife's red Saab along the highway with my two little girls in the back seat. I was headed for work, and my daughters were on their way to visit their old babysitter.

The heater appeared to be blowing cold air, and I wanted to make my girls warmer. I thought I may have somehow inadvertently pushed the air conditioning button on, so I took my eyes off the road for *just a second* to look for it and press it off.

My eyes left the road for just *one* second.

When I looked up again, we had drifted to the left shoulder of the highway. I moved the wheel to the right to ease back onto the road and the front left wheel dropped into the grass median. The long, low front end of the Saab caught the shoulder, and the car began flipping over and over and over in the median at sixty miles per hour.

As we hurtled through space, my daughter Stefanie was screaming, "Daddy, what's happening? Daddy, what's happening?" But I couldn't answer her.

I watched in terror—arms flailing, everything moving as if in slow motion—as the sunroof tore away, and frozen earth and debris scraped in through the open hatch each time the sky was below us. The windows blew out, and the roof on the front passenger side—above the only empty seat—collapsed, but we were still flying.

Then, there was silence. The car was still. I turned to see Stefanie, cowered in the corner and whimpering, but alive and whole. I twisted around a little more to see her little sister, Madeline, who was strapped in behind me. I couldn't see her face because it was covered in blood. While both girls made it through, the image of the red stains on

Madeline's little yellow ski jacket is still vivid in my memory.

Six months before the accident, I had visited my doctor to express concern about a little bleeding problem of my own. Jeffrey had recommended that I visit a gastroenterologist for one of those invasive exams that men, in particular, will do anything to avoid. And so, I avoided it. Now, having survived that accident, I finally found the courage to go for the exam. That's how, one month after the accident, I learned that I had colon cancer.

From that moment on, our lives began flipping over and over like that red Saab: extensive surgery at Memorial Sloan Kettering Cancer Center, learning that the disease had already begun to spread, a devastating course of chemotherapy, the cold, sterile radiation therapy room, bouts of abdominal pain so severe that my frightened children found me crawling on my hands and knees, hospitalizations for morphine, coming within hours of death, a second extensive surgery at Sloan Kettering—this time to save my life.

Twice, I was blessed to be able to leave Memorial Sloan Kettering Cancer Center and return home. Each time I left a roommate who never made it back to *his* home. By August, my weight had dropped from a healthy 155 pounds to 112 and the complications that made the second surgery necessary had left me totally disabled.

I couldn't work, we were bankrupt, and even my most loyal clients could not wait to see if I'd ever be there for them again.

My struggle over the next few years to create a new life—one filled with adventure, passion and joy—taught me lessons about mastering fear that I have been sharing ever since. They became part of my first book, *The High Diving Board*. Among other things, I learned how easy it is to delude yourself into believing you've climbed all the steps to your high diving board, when you've really just settled at a lower board somewhere along the path.

I wrote the book and became a business and life coach because I believe that my survival was a gift. If I can help even just a few people propel themselves up the path that leads to *their* high diving board, I survived for a purpose.

Recently, I was tested a second time; this time it was prostate cancer that had broken through the wall of the prostate but hadn't reached the lymph nodes. It's been twenty-one years and I've been relatively healthy since my recovery, but it seems that when I do develop a problem, I do it in a big way. More surgery and more complications but for now, it looks like I'm out of the woods again.

Purpose is powerful medicine. It can't necessarily prevent illness, but it can inspire you to get up again and again. If your purpose is serving others, it's the most powerful medicine of all.

Sandy Schussel left his law practice, worked his way into a position as the National Sales Training Director for an investment/insurance company, and eventually found his ideal career as a business and life coach specializing in performance and leadership issues for business owners and sales professionals. He is also a motivational speaker and the author of two acclaimed books, The High Diving Board: How to Overcome Your Fears and Live Your Dreams *and* Become a Client Magnet: 27 Strategies to Boost Your Client Attraction Factor.

> *"If you think you can do a thing or think you can't do a thing, you're right."*
> - Henry Ford

Raised by Wolves

Mark Crowley

I was raised by wolves.

There's no literal truth to this statement and yet it feels accurate as an explanation for the inhuman and often heartless care I received during most of my childhood. Ironically, wolves have quite a good reputation for rearing their young; had wolves really raised me, I'm inclined to believe their nurturing instincts would've been far superior to those of the humans who did raise me. They would almost have to be.

One of my brothers is certain my father's intention was to *destroy* the lives of all his children. While I've never wanted to accept this assertion as truth (who wants to believe that of their own father?), the psychic wounds we all suffered were too numerous, deep and enduring to argue otherwise.

My father was a man who almost never conveyed his love or esteem for me.

Instead, starting when I was very little, he went to work on dismantling my sense of well-being. Some inner directive made him destructive in his approach to motivating my behavior and achievement.

He was an extremely volatile person who came home from work almost every night enraged. Although I tried, nothing I did could ever please him. This was dispiriting to me as a young boy, of course, but it was the way he chose to express his displeasure that did the most harm. He would scream. The reverberation of his yelling undoubtedly did cellular damage to me, but even more injurious were the things he said—things he wanted me to believe about myself and to know he believed about me. Using ten-dollar words that pierced, my father took direct hits on my equilibrium and self-confidence.

To convey his belief that I lacked ambition, he called me *shiftless*. He told me I was *mendacious* (a liar), an *ingrate* and had *no milk of human kindness*. He characterized me as being *pusillanimous*, meaning he saw me as having a contemptible lack of boldness and resolve. I didn't even know the meaning of his expressions when I first heard them, but the venomous intonation he used conveyed their inherent meaning.

He used the Latin phrase, *Non compos mentis,* to assert that I had an inferior mind but relied upon the King's English to more accessibly communicate his lack of confidence in me. For years he forecasted that mine would be a life of failure, telling me I would never measure up and that I would never amount to anything. I learned from him that whatever I did, whoever I would become, in his eyes, I would never be enough.

While it's a mystery to me why I was born to be parented by someone so dysfunctional and abusive, it's also curious that a safe haven—an alternative universe— was placed in the house right next door. When I was nine years old, my mother died and my father remarried. My new stepmother was indifferent and unwelcoming and insisted I spend little time at home. I was effectively forced to find someplace else to go after school each day.

I chose to go next door because my two best friends lived there. It didn't seem to matter to their mother that, all of a sudden, I was coming over *every* day and staying until very late. Knowing I had almost nowhere else to go, this greatly heartened me. But a form of spiritual fireworks exploded inside me when my friends' mother told me that I was not only welcome in her home but that she *wanted* me there. Soon, she was laughing at my jokes, taking an interest in my schoolwork, and soliciting my observations about the world. More than anything, she validated what I wanted to believe was my real truth—that I was a great kid with wonderful potential. Her generous, thoughtful and consistent gestures of care, encouragement and validation sustained me over many years and made an enormous difference to my surviving such an insane ordeal.

When I turned eighteen, my father kicked me out of the house. Even with all of the disharmony in our home, his decision caught me by complete surprise. It had never crossed my mind that he wouldn't support me while I attended college. But he didn't. While quite wealthy, he offered no financial assistance. He provided no direction or guidance. I moved into an apartment and into five of the most difficult and stressful years of my life. Not once did he check in to see if I was holding up.

I found new friends who routinely assured me I would endure and succeed. They empathized with what I was going through and found ways to show their care. Part of my motivation to get through college was to prove to myself that my father had been wrong about me. That's a corrupt motivation, of course, and one driven by fear and feelings of unworthiness. However, my success had much more to do with the professors, bosses and other people in my life who saw my potential and made impactful gestures of care at just the right moments. What an enormous difference those things made in my life.

It's been over thirty years since the end of my childhood and it's taken a long part of that time for me to make complete peace with all I endured growing up. But in the end, I came to more than just accept and forgive all that occurred. I came to believe it all happened for a reason—for a *purpose*.

I believe I had the childhood experiences I did for the purpose of discovering a more productive and sustainable way of relating to and leading people, a new and transformational model that inspires people to perform and contribute to their highest potential all the while ensuring *all* constituencies—employers, shareholders and workers—routinely flourish.

Much like children in the Great Depression whose early deprivation influenced them to scrimp and save for the rest of their lives, my severe upbringing changed my original wiring. It made me more sensitive to people and gave me unusual insight into what people needed to thrive. All the abuse and fundamental lack of support led me to treat more humanely those people I supervised and to find ways of maximizing their talents. All the years I was growing up, I used to fantasize about how much more of my potential could have been realized had I been better cared for and more thoughtfully directed. Knowing all the things I felt I had missed out on—and always had wanted—I made the decision to give those things to others.

What I chose to do is basic and fundamental—but quite uncommon in business. I nurtured and supported the human needs in people so they could perform to their greatest potential. I did this unconsciously at first and all my teams excelled. For many years, I took the success for granted and didn't connect the dots. But after several years passed and I had the experience of leading myriad business units and teams of people, it became quite evident that the leadership practices I implemented in response to a profoundly painful childhood were influencing people to be remarkably engaged and high achieving.

When I first sat down to write my book, I had a very straightforward ambition: to share those four specific leadership practices that I found had the most powerful effect on people and inspired their highest engagement and productivity. But as I closed myself off and began real consideration into what I would write, I dug deeper into the question of *why* these practices had been so effective on other people. I had always known that they worked but my original motivation for employing them was because I believed they would have worked for *me*.

Inevitably, I came to understand that what I had been doing all along was positively affecting people's hearts. I realized that people had responded to this kind of leadership because they felt I was someone who genuinely cared and who made an effort to express that to them. People sensed that who they were and what they contributed was valued, and these feelings motivated them to perform at extraordinary levels.

My epiphany was that I had brought heart into leadership, and this revelation stopped me in my tracks.

The idea of leading with *any* amount of heart flies in the face of our collective belief that the heart acts like kryptonite in business. We associate the heart in the workplace as being soft, sentimental and antithetical to driving profit. We frown on heart. In the moment, I was greatly conflicted. I knew from my own twenty-five years of leadership experience that people had scaled the tallest mountains for me because I recognized their individual genius, helped them to develop it, put it to its best use and helped them to find gratification in the work they did. There was no question in my mind that heart had been the *catalyst* for their exceptional achievement.

We've been led to believe the mind is the highest form of intelligence possible and rarely think to consult the heart as we work to motivate people to perform. We've groomed our leaders to be intellectual, to subordinate feeling and to marginalize their hearts. However, this mind-driven belief system is flawed. It disconnects leaders from the people they lead and limits their effectiveness.

What I've learned and concluded is that we need a new model of leadership for a new age—a paradigm that acknowledges the humanity—the hearts—in people. To be very clear and direct, this is by no means a feel-good strategy. It's based on our collective understanding that it's rarely, if ever, an appeal to our *minds* that inspires any of us to do our greatest work. It's also based upon the understanding that when people flourish, organizations flourish. It can be condensed to these two sentences from a Scandinavian proverb: "In every man there is a king. Speak to the king and the king will come forth."

Mark C. Crowley is a leadership consultant, speaker and author whose mission is to fundamentally change how we lead and manage people in the 21st-century workplace.

> *"Good luck is another name for tenacity of purpose."*
> --Ralph Waldo Emerson

We Are Not Alone

Meredith O'Connor

By the time I was 14, I was constantly bullied about being too tall and too thin. There were days when classmates literally spit on me, and when the kids at my school played the "Would You Rather" game, it wasn't unusual to offer the choice of an unpleasant death or doing something intimate with me. The bullying was so bad that I developed an anxiety disorder in middle school. Ironically, it was during this time that I was discovered by City Model Management and soon after signed by a record label.

It was confusing being told I was ugly at school but being told I was pretty at photo shoots. Being a victim of bullying can have long-lasting consequences, but I found the most closure once I spoke out about it. After my song "Celebrity" went viral, I had a meeting with the label. I was in a room full of strangers when my manager suggested that I write a song about something I had gone through. The song I wrote was "The Game."

After "The Game" came out, I received messages and letters from thousands of fans telling me how they experienced bullying and similar trauma. This taught me that I wasn't alone; bullying happens to millions of people around the world. I also realized that I had been so afraid to talk about it because I was the victim of abuse, and like any victim, I was afraid to speak out. I encourage fans to recognize they are a victim of abuse whenever I can. I do this in the hopes that they will not blame themselves for what happened or buy into what the bullies say. This helps them realize they can take other actions—like telling someone they trust—rather than hurting themselves or turning to suicide.

We need to take bullying seriously. As someone who suffered from it, I can tell you it causes mental scarring, anxiety, and post-traumatic stress disorder and can trigger OCD. The thing that got me through it all was telling myself that one day it would get better, and that one day I would wake up and my dreams would come true.

When I'm singing to a sold-out crowd or flying across the world, sometimes I have to pinch myself and remember how lucky I am. So many of my fans have talent and beauty that is being shut down. Seeing them believe what these bullies say, the same way I once did, truly hurts me. Improving one's self-esteem takes work and perseverance. Sometimes, if you can't figure out how to love yourself, you can first find an external passion to drive you and through that you learn how to love yourself. This is a good place to start and was how I began my own journey into recovery. I told myself it would get better and focused on my passion for music and performing and saw much more success than I ever expected. Seeing a doctor and finally opening up about the anxiety disorder that stemmed from the abuse at school taught me to rewire my own brain, eliminating anxiety and shutting up the fear that threatened my healing process. It really made me grow up fast. A lot of times people forget my age. I am still growing and learning, so the responsibilities that come with the spotlight and position I'm in can seem overwhelming sometimes, but I have learned to surround myself with good people. One thing that I remind myself, and that you should remember too, is that we aren't alone and we can get through this.

*"Strength does not come from winning.
Your struggles develop your strengths.
When you go through hardships and
decide not to surrender,
that is strength."*
—Arnold Schwarzenegger

Finding Positivity after Tragedy

Girish Gogia

In 1999, I was at a beach in Goa to usher in the millennium. A confident ocean diver, I took off over the side of a cliff. Unfortunately, this was a miscalculated dive that changed my life completely. Since then, I have been totally paralyzed from the neck down due to a cervical spinal cord injury that left all my limbs immobile and resulted in 50 percent respiratory function, failure of bladder, no bowel movements, and zero sensation in almost 90 percent of my body. I wondered why I was chosen for such a fate. WHY ME?

In spite of all the resulting physical limitations, day-to-day challenges, and adversities, I make it a point to live life with a smile and a positive attitude. I am blessed by Almighty God with a lot of positive energy. I am not what happened to me. I am what I choose to become!

My wife Eesha suffers from multiple sclerosis, is 70 percent paralyzed, and has been bedridden for the last seven years. She also makes it a point to motivate and inspire people all around her. In spite of the challenges we both face each day, we have not given up hope. We finally realized the true purpose of our lives and decided to share our real-life experiences as well as our positive energy and let people know about their own untapped potential

I realize I may not be who I ought to be. I know that I'm not all that I want to be. However, I have come a long way from who I used to be, and I won't give up on what I know I can be. That's why I began my journey as a motivational and inspirational speaker traveling around the globe conducting workshops, spreading happiness and positivity, and making it a point to put smiles on every face. I will continue doing so until I take my last breath.

By the grace of the Almighty, the title of "The Positive Man" was bestowed upon me by *The Times of India*. I was also awarded the Karamveer Chakra Medallion by the Indian Confederation of NGOs and given the prestigious Positive Health Hero Award in 2013 by Indian superstar Hrithik Roshan, an award organized by Dr. Batra's Foundation.

I wish to emphasize that I am very passionate and have a tremendous amount of unconditional love and respect for each and every human. I consider this mission as my moral responsibility, my duty as a human being. It seems God himself chose me as a small messenger to spread the positive energy around. I realize that we all die. The goal isn't to live forever. The goal is to create something that will live forever. This thought came to me as a divine intervention seven years back.

In spite of all the trials, I didn't allow hope to cease. I realized that nothing was impossible. It was all about the indomitable spirit and mind over matter. Through my trials and tribulations, I discovered that a positive, passionate, and progressive attitude helped me excavate myself from the morasses of life and proceed positively. I realized that the time had come to act, instead of sulking.

Fortunately, I have always known for sure that what lies behind me and what lies in front of me bear very little resemblance to what lies inside of me. As author Ralph Parlette said, "All outside greatness is merely an incidental reflection of the inside." I went through hundreds of hours of self-talking and self-realization. I used to say things to myself like, "Hey, just take a look, there is a real gold mine inside. Look at yourself, you are perfectly fine. Just focus on the vital organs of your body, which are still functioning fine. There is absolutely no need to concentrate on what is not working." I promised myself that I wouldn't allow any negative thoughts to rent space in my head. So I made it a point to raise the rent and kick them out!"

I knew that all I needed to do was to dive deep and dig into my infinite resources of positive energy, passion, determination, and willpower. I knew that every human being has power and potential beyond imagination and that every human is born to succeed. Of all the challenges we face, we can either flourish or perish. So we must face the challenges head on. We are an amazing piece of technology. We are designed for accomplishment, engineered for success, and endowed with the spirit of greatness. We are all born to win; we just have to believe it. We have to believe in the tremendous magic and greatness that resides in all the trillions of cells in our minds and bodies. I had to tap that reservoir of hidden potential inside me. I thought about these things thousands of times each day. The very fact that I have been gifted with the life of a human being and not any other species in itself means that I stand at the top of the millions of species living on this planet.

I also realized that nothing truly stops you. Nothing truly holds you back. Your own will is always within your control. So I firmly decided not to give up and to overcome each and every painful task. I knew that doing so would only take me ahead in life.

The realization that limitations are imaginary made me much stronger and more powerful. I had this burning desire to accomplish my ideas no matter what, and that's what it takes to achieve anything in life. That scorching, sizzling inferno deep within my heart made me achieve my dreams. I understood that the human spirit is stronger than anything that can happen to the body. We are the creators of our own destiny. If we want to make our dreams come true, the first thing we have to do is wake up. Someone once asked me how I keep moving forward after all the adversities and trying times that I've been through. I replied that it's because no matter what happens, I'm a survivor and not a victim.

I had always heard that heroes are those who believed they could do something when no one else did. They were those who chose to fight rather than give up, those whose lives became a message to inspire the ages. I wanted to be such a hero. I had such a wonderful opportunity to change the future, not only for myself but also for those millions across the globe that I unconditionally love and respect. An opportunity to create a life filled with passion, inspiration, and purpose. Discovering the true me was closer than I ever thought. Discovering the real me was within my reach.

Today, enduring setbacks while maintaining the ability to show others the way forward is truly satisfying and gives me eternal happiness. What looked like the biggest loss of my life turned out to be the very event that helped to produce the major achievement of my life. Our problems are really our blessings if we use them to grow stronger.

As a human being, I feel it is my duty to share my experiences with others and convey the message of positivity. Hence I have undertaken this mission to enlighten as many souls as possible through the power of positive energy, motivational workshops, motivational lectures, and life-transforming sessions to change their perception toward life.

I sincerely feel that I have been blessed by the Almighty and can help people achieve peak performance by tapping the dormant nuclear reactor within to take them on a high-speed cruise to their ultimate potential. It is my goal to make every soul realize they are not just a drop in the ocean, but are themselves an ocean within that very drop. I live my life by the Confucius quote: "Our greatest glory is not in never falling, but in rising every time we fall."

Girish Gogia is known as The Positive Man. A civil engineer by qualification and an interior designer by profession, he is now a motivational and inspirational speaker focused on spreading the power of positive energy across the globe.

> *"A hero is an ordinary individual who finds the strength to persevere and endure in spite of overwhelming obstacles."*
> --Christopher Reeve

Giving, Receiving and Respecting Love

Sharyel

This isn't about me—this is about bringing awareness to others. I love life and there is no doubt about that, but what I love even more is using my experience to teach others to avoid the situation I found myself in.

It was February 2011. I was in the shower when it happened. I found the lump on my left breast. I went to my gynecologist and he decided to do a breast biopsy first. The breast biopsy results were in within a week. It was then that I learned I had cancer. Receiving that phone call from my GYN was devastating. Little did I know the journey ahead would be a war and that I would literally have to fight for my life to win.

After receiving the diagnosis, I was referred to an oncology surgeon who gave me the option of a lumpectomy or mastectomy with or without reconstruction. I chose a lumpectomy to preserve my breast—

it was important for me to continue to feel like a woman. In March I had the lumpectomy to remove the 3 cm lump, and it was found that I had stage 2A breast cancer.

In April, a port catheter was inserted into my chest just above my left breast in order to begin chemo. Not everyone receives chemo with stage 2A cancer, but my tumor was a grade 3. This is the most aggressive grade, which dictated that chemo was needed.

I had chemo treatments until September. This was a rough time. I received chemo every three weeks. The first week after treatment I was in so much pain, there was no question I was staying in bed. The second week, I was able to do a little bit of work from home. The third week I was still rundown but found myself able to go into the office to work. Unfortunately, after that third week, the process started all over again with a new round of chemo.

I wanted to keep my figure just like every woman would, so I chose to do breast preservation ... originally. After chemo, I was instructed to go through 37 rounds of radiation. Radiation happened five days a week until the 37 rounds were complete.

Radiation took its toll on my whole body, but especially the breast that was originally affected with the cancer. The breast became inflamed, swollen and had the texture of an orange peel. It was then that I decided that nipples were overrated and I had to get rid of what was killing me.

After the orange-peel scare, I decided to have a double mastectomy, which is called a bilateral mastectomy. I also chose to do reconstruction. Both the oncologist and plastic surgeon worked together to perform both surgeries at the same time. The oncologist removed my breast while the plastic surgeon came right behind him and did a latissimus dorsi reconstruction. The plastic surgeon relocated two of the largest muscles in my back through my armpits to the front of my new breast. This was to be the foundation and structure for my new breasts. He placed tissue expanders under the skin that the first surgeon left. These expanders were filled with saline and would continue to be filled with saline for a period of two weeks. Once the desired size was acquired, the expenders would be left in place for nine months. When the nine months passed, I underwent another surgery to replace the expanders with silicone implants. Right now I am awaiting nipple reconstruction. Currently I have transplanted skin that also came from my back; this will become nipples after the plastic surgeon works his magic. The areolae will come from a skin graft taken from my thighs at the same time he does the nipples. Several months after the new nipples heal, I will get them tattooed to match my original nipples in color and size. Then the reconstruction will be complete.

Chemo also worked its wonders at sparking up my childhood asthma. Now I have severe asthma that I am hospitalized for often. I see a doctor almost once a week, whether it's for my asthma, fever or my cancer. Most recently, the doctors found a mass on my ovary … my remaining ovary, that is. The doctors were concerned that it was my breast cancer finding itself a new location in my beat-down body. Breast cancer doesn't stay in the breast; it spreads like a weed to different locations in your body including the liver, bone, ovaries, etc. The removal of my last ovary meant that my body was no longer producing estrogen, which is what my type of breast cancer was feeding on.

Throughout my struggle with cancer came loneliness. I lost my husband earlier in my life, as he was in the military. I'm fortunate to have my daughter live with me, but I know that she has a life and job of her own and cannot be my full-time caregiver. My son is away at college trying to make a life for himself. I am proud of my children and would not want to tie them down with my illnesses. I want to see them succeed in this beautiful world without this devilish disease.

I was blessed with another person in my life who came during my time of need. She was from my church family and has become true family. She is a year older than my daughter and a full-time college student. It started with her not having a place to stay during the few months she wasn't attending college, so I allowed her to stay with me. She is still with me after two years and shows care and love for me each day. She calls me mommy, just like my other two children. She was often my helper, taking me to doctor's appointments and emergency appointments, and constantly makes sure I have what I need when I need it. I tell people I have three kids: two girls and one boy. She is just as special as my biological children. They are all blessings in my life.

I was lucky enough to have my church support me through this tough time. Whether they were cooking, cleaning or simply being there for me, I knew I could call them my church family. As I casually talked to my doctor about how lonely I felt, I mentioned thinking about getting a dog to keep me company. He thought this was a great idea, that it would be therapeutic. It just so happened that his boxer had puppies at that time. I found myself taking one of these puppies to have as my own. I named him Socrates.

Socrates is what I fight for now. I know that when I'm in the hospital, I have to fight to get back to him. He is my determination. I miss him and he misses me. There is no tearing this team apart. This is more than just owning a dog; this is owning a reason to keep going, no matter how tough it gets.

As I mentioned, my church family became part of my real family during this time. Would you go through an illness like this and want your family members to suffer from the same thing? I feel it is my responsibility to bring awareness to whoever will listen to me. Once, during the month of October, my church allowed me to find a speaker to bring awareness of breast cancer. Each October, we try to get the whole congregation to wear pink to show support. I'm willing to do anything to prevent my church family from falling to the same disease I did. I want to be their prevention.

Did you know that men and children are also vulnerable to breast cancer? I want to make people feel comfortable with checking themselves and their children for lumps in their breasts. The longer you let it go, the more serious it gets. Please don't let this awful disease consume your body. Prevent it from doing so by checking yourself and advise your loved ones to do the same.

This whole experience has been very tough, but it is now my duty to bring awareness to absolutely everyone about this disease. I also know that no matter what, I now have a greater appreciation for life, family and friends. Friends come through in your time of need. During this whole experience, I've never once been neglected or ignored. I have a new appreciation for each day, no matter the pain and difficulties I go through. If I can go through this tough time and still find time to praise God, you can too. Don't forget to praise God.

When I was asked to share my story in this book, a woman asked me, "What have you taken from your experiences thus far?" I became emotional and replied, "Love, love, love. Give love, receive love, respect love." I had the experience of almost passing on; I saw how my family and friends reacted and how my passing on would affect them. I saw the effect that I can have on the world. I want everyone to know that you will go where you are intended to go. If you go, you have served your purpose. This is why awareness is so big to me; I want everyone to have as many chances as possible to serve their purpose. Don't cut your chances of serving your purpose; cut your chances of dying from breast cancer by checking yourself regularly.

If you take one thing from my story, have it be love. Give love, receive love, respect love.

"Strength and growth come only through continuous effort and struggle."
--Napoleon Hill

Never Stop Believing

Rae

In the Charlie Brown cartoon strip, there's a character called Pigpen. He has a dark halo of dust and dirt that always follows him. When I describe my depression and how it feels around me, I think of Pigpen. When I'm depressed, it constantly feels like I'm in a dark, messy cloud through which I can't see where I'm going. My head is a mess, and I don't think rationally. It's a constant, everyday battle.

After attending counseling in college, I realized that at age 13 I'd had my first depressive episode. At that time, I had just lost my grandma, who was like a mother to me. She, my grandpa and I were very close, and they took care of me. The effect of her loss was devastating, especially since I had a poor relationship with my parents. As a result, I got into my first unhealthy relationship. I was not ready to be sexually active, but the guy I was dating was ready.

He was forceful when I didn't want to do things. During this phase, I had a very verbally abusive relationship with my parents, and I was bullied. Due to the many contributing factors, I looked for any way to diminish the pain, and I resorted to cutting myself. I would scrape myself with any sharp object I could find and keep going until I was raw and bleeding because I wanted to feel a different pain than what I was going through.

I was also bulimic off and on from eighth grade until my junior year of high school. I looked for pills that would help me overdose. I didn't want to die, but I was just so scared, lost and alone. There was only one time I contemplated taking my own life. I had written out a suicide note, gotten a knife, and sat on my bedroom floor with it, crying hysterically. I thank God every day that I didn't go through with it.

During my freshman year of high school I ended the unhealthy relationship and was in a much better mental state than I had been the previous year, but I was still battling many insecurities. On the bright side, I had two best friends with whom I spent a lot of time, until my ex came into the picture. He was 18 while I was 14. We soon became sexually active, and then after three months of dating, he broke up with me. During the time I was with him, I drank very heavily. One night after we were broken up, I was drinking with a friend. My ex and his friend ended up coming over. Although I had been somewhat sexually active up to now, I'd never had intercourse. I lost my virginity that night and barely have memory of it. My ex was also dating another girl at the time, so losing my virginity to him meant absolutely nothing. I was very emotionally hurt; I felt used, dirty and stupid.

At 14, I turned to alcohol to help ease the pain of my mistake. I got drunk any time I could. Because of the alcohol, I ended up being sexually active with three more guys, one who used me just for sex for an entire year. I hated myself and how I looked, but I thought that being with a guy sexually would lead to a relationship in which someone else would love me so I could learn to love myself. This was a belief that followed me all the way to college.

College was a blur of bad relationships, depression and countless one-night stands to find love in all the wrong places. I was extremely insecure, had no self-respect and I just wanted to feel something when I had one-night stands. I slept with a lot of men, but only five that I actually consented to and wanted to happen. The rest were drunken nights where I would be saying, "No, we shouldn't do this," or, "No, I don't really want to." I didn't scream *no* during any of these times, but no means no, no matter what form it comes in.

During this phase of my sophomore year in college, I went to the doctor and found out I had herpes. Every pain, insecurity and horrible feeling I had ever felt resurfaced and felt like a hurricane hitting me. I continued to drink heavily and blacked out most nights; I also slept with about seven people after I got the diagnosis, due to being so intoxicated. I felt horrible, and all I wanted to do was die.

A few months after finding out about the herpes diagnosis, I realized I could no longer live my life this way—I needed help. But I hated help. I didn't want to admit to anything. I was trying to be independent and fix all of my problems myself. Eventually, I gave in and called the counseling center where I meant Anna.

The next two years were a rocky rollercoaster ride to say the least. Through counseling I learned I was severely depressed and an alcoholic. While going there I got better, happier and things really started to look up for me.

Shortly after summer, I stopped going to counseling because Anna moved. I relapsed into old habits and was drinking excessively and having unwanted hookups. I became more depressed than I had ever been. My relationship with my parents was awful. I felt unloved, unwanted, dirty, tainted and I hated myself for what I'd gotten myself into. I was always very against antidepressants due to the effects I saw them have on my mother, so I tried counseling again, which is where I meant Leila. I still felt miserable and my life was becoming unbearable. I didn't want to do anything except be alone. After multiple hysterical crying episodes with my best friend, she insisted that I give medication a try.

I started Prozac and my biggest fear came true. The medicine actually made me feel worse. I was on it for two weeks and was having anxiety attacks and feeling like I just wanted to die. I got off of it right away and never wanted to try medication again. Two close friends and my teacher pushed me to try again with something different. I thank God every day that I did because I FINALLY found happiness.

I have been on Lexapro for five months, and it has probably been the best five months of my life. I'm proud to say that my life is finally heading in a direction that allows me to become a much better person than I ever could have imagined. The medicine did not make me feel like a superwoman, but it allowed me to cope with things in my life in a rational manner. The perspective I have now is extremely different, and that's what really saved me. When a person is depressed, they truly don't realize how bad or miserable they are because that is the lifestyle they are accustomed to. It becomes a normal, everyday occurrence to feel the dark cloud swarming around.

Looking back on everything that has happened to me and seeing how far I have come, I owe my biggest thanks to my best friend, her family, my teacher, my counselor and most importantly, God. God never gave up on me, even when I gave up on myself. He was always that little voice in my head pushing me to do more, to better myself, to go to counseling and give medication a try. He never stopped being there for me. I always thought that anyone I got close to and opened up to would end up leaving me, but I have realized that I have NEVER been alone. God has been with me every single step in my journey, holding my hand in the process. I know I have had many struggles, but I also know God's plan for my life is bigger than I ever could have imagined.

That is why I am hopeful, faithful and happy with life now because I know all the pain I have experienced served a very purposeful meaning in my life. Never stop believing God loves and is always with you.

"You have power over your mind - not outside events. Realize this, and you will find strength."
--Marcus Aurelius

Still Going Strong

Micayla Fitzsimmons

Here I sit, twenty-two years old, engaged to Brandon Ordway. We will welcome our bundle of joy, Miss Kailyn, in mid-June. I never thought my life would take me to this place.

Let's rewind my life back to July 2001. I was nine years old. July 14 was the last time I ever saw my dad. He and my mother dropped both my sister Cassi and me off at our Grandma and Grandpa Buntain's house. My parents had plans for Sunday morning to help some friends out. I was upset as they left, and I remember telling them both I hated them and proceeded to cry. I loved spending time with my mom and dad; there was nothing I enjoyed more. I settled down once they left and soon it was time for bed.

I woke the next morning to go to church with my grandparents and sister, just like any other Sunday that we stayed there. Typical routine—breakfast, then drive to church and then to Big Boy restaurant. However, this day the routine was broken. As we pulled into Big Boy, I noticed my dad's friend's truck sitting there. My first thought was that Mom and Dad showed up to eat with us. My dad's friend tried to get my grandpa out of the van, but he refused to get out. Instead, my grandma got out to talk to them. She started to cry, and Grandpa told us kids that we would not be eating breakfast that morning. At this point, I was very confused, probably the most confused I have ever been in my life.

We headed back to my grandparents' house. Shortly after we got there, many family members showed up—aunts, uncles and cousins. Then my mom arrived, her eye makeup dripping down her face, tears filling her eyes. We sat down in the kitchen—I was on my mom's lap, and we were told dad was not coming back. He had been killed. Even at the age of nine, I was lost. Family members tried to keep our spirits up by taking us out to the pool and keeping us busy. I had no interest in being anywhere but with my mom.

Having my world turned upside down at such a young age has been one the hardest things life has thrown my way. Our mom did everything in her power to keep Cassi and me happy. With the tremendous help of our grandparents, we did okay. Life was different but we made it work, somehow.

Fast-forward to when I was sixteen, twenty days until my seventeenth birthday, at Cassi's senior year choir concert where only the best singers got to perform with others from the state. Mom, Grandma, Grandpa and I made the trip to Toledo to watch her perform. Her group was the second out of three. Her performance was over at nine and since I had to be at school the next day, my mom decided to take me home, leaving Grandma and Grandpa to bring Cassi home once she was allowed to leave.

We'd just pulled in the driveway when my mom received a call from my sister's cell phone. I heard nothing but crying and sirens on the other end as my mom tried to calm down Cassi. Mom hung up the phone and said we had to go back to Toledo immediately. Grandpa had suffered a heart attack, and they were leaving the theater via ambulance. It was about eleven when we pulled into University of Toledo Hospital. It was several hours before we could see Grandpa, the longest hours of my life.

Over the next eighteen days, countless trips were made to Toledo as they kept him in ICU. March 19 rolled around and they told us they were going to transfer him to a nursing home in Defiance where they would slowly start some rehab. It was easier to have him close to home—less stress on everybody.

The morning of my birthday, March 21, arrived. I had plans with my cousin to go out to eat and then visit my grandpa at the nursing home. Once she picked me up, I asked her if we could switch up the plans and go see Grandpa first. We headed to Twin Rivers and walked into his room. Grandma was excited to see me on my birthday. I walked over to Grandpa and he gave me a kiss, as per usual. I walked back over to talk with my grandma. As I did, my grandpa's machines began making unusual noises. Nurses rushed into the room and started talking to my grandma, asking if they should resuscitate. She told them no; he had asked to only be resuscitated once.

I heard my grandma telling him it was okay, she would be okay, telling him if he needed to go, then go. I found myself backing up all the way into the hallway. I watched his skin turn from normal, to yellow, to white. I realized I had just watched my grandpa pass away. The rock of our family had just left us. I had no idea what to think. I was angry, I was scared, I was lost again. The four of us—Grandma, my mom, my sister and me—became closer than ever.

In 2011, my mother started having health issues and it took until March to get her to agree to go to a doctor. Two days after my birthday, she was given the news that pancreatic cancer had taken over about seventy percent of her liver. After more appointments, she was told she had six months to live without treatment, maybe up to a year with treatment. In April, she was given the option of doing a trial drug they nicknamed "hedgehog." Her exact words were, "Although this will probably not help my case, it can help others, and that's why I will participate in this." Such courage and strength she had.

She was to start her trial drug usage on April 18, but complications started on the fourteenth. She had slept until about one in the afternoon, was up until about five, then had to lie back down. She slept until about ten at night, and we all decided to wake her up since she'd been asleep all day. We noticed she was not making any sense, asking what day it was, and she just wasn't quite with it. I walked with her to the living room, where she collapsed. We finally talked her into calling the ambulance, and they took her to Defiance Regional Medical Center. There we were met by an abundance of family members. The doctors could not come up with an answer about what was going on other than a fever and an infection somewhere. She elected to go to University of Michigan where her cancer doctor was located. The next two days were nothing but stressful. Test after test after test, the family was taken into a room to talk with doctors, who told us the infection was nowhere that they had looked and that the next step would be to look in spots that would force her to be on a ventilator. There was no promise she would ever come off it or that they would even find where the infection was. Why? Why put her through that without knowing we would get an answer?

Mom wanted us included in the decision, so Cassi and I had to decide whether to try more treatment or let the infection take over. For a nineteen- and twenty-year-old who have already lost a tremendous amount of close family, we couldn't bear to lose another, but we couldn't put her in pain. We decided it was time to let God do his thing and take her when she was ready. We went into her room, our eyes full of tears, and let her know what we thought she should do. She smiled that beautiful smile that's still on everyone's mind. She had two requests: one, to not feel death, and two, to be buried with our dad.

The next day, she became unresponsive because of the medications they had her on so she would not feel a thing. They noticed she was just hanging on with everything she had. We decided to transport her back to Defiance—maybe being closer to home would magically do the work. We got her to hospice care in Defiance on April 16. The whole night she had visitors, pouring into the next day. On the night of the seventeenth, after giving her multiple kisses and holding her hand (though she was unconscious), I had to pull myself away to relax. My grandma, sister and aunt decided to stay the night with her. My aunt had asked if anything happened if I wanted her to call me; I said absolutely.

Going to bed was difficult, knowing the phone would probably ring. About four in the morning I woke up out of nowhere and not a minute later, my phone rang. I burst into tears knowing I didn't want to answer it. My aunt on the other line explained that Mom was no longer in pain and had joined my dad and grandpa. I broke down, and as I hung up, I asked myself, "Why? What do I do now?"

With everything that has happened in my life, I have found the one question, *why*, to be the one I never get answered, but what they say is true. God never gives you anything you cannot handle. Maybe you can't handle it on your own, but there will be people there for you to help even when you feel like it's the world versus you. Anger and questioning your faith is common. But keeping trust in the Lord, that He has a greater plan for you, is key.

Being twenty-two and about to start a family of my own is an amazing feeling. Knowing I have all these guardian angels is what keeps me going. Knowing they really are watching over me and sensing them each time I catch the smell of lavender, see a butterfly or a beautiful sunset, reassures me they are okay. Never give up hope and trust in the Lord when you think it can't get better. Know that it does get better. It might not be tomorrow or next week, but it comes. Never be afraid to cry; it does not mean you are weak. It simply means you've been too strong for too long and there is nothing wrong with that.

My name is Micayla Fitzsimmons, and my world has been turned upside down, sideways and inside out since I was nine. I find hope in family and friends, and I'm still going strong.

*"All the adversity I've had in my life, all
my troubles and obstacles, have
strengthened me...
You may not realize it when it happens,
but a kick in the teeth may be the best
thing in the world for you."*
--Walt Disney

Staying Strong and Moving On

Bailey

Without my knowledge, my father molested my half-brothers, who were his stepchildren. By the time my mother found out, she was separated from my father. At that point, my half-brothers had already molested most of our male and female cousins—but I didn't know that. My mother took her anger out on me emotionally and physically while also neglecting my basic needs.

After my eighth-grade graduation, I fell into a predator's hands. This man was twenty-five and abused me sexually, physically and mentally. I lost contact with my family and didn't even make it to high school because he wouldn't let me leave his sight.

A few years later I ended up pregnant. I loved my little girl and got her out of that situation. I started talking to my mom and half-brothers. When I did, my mother seemed very caring and sincere. I believed she was a changed person. I still had no knowledge of any sexual abuse involving my half-brothers. I let my mother take my daughter some weekends, as I had to work. Without my consent or knowledge, she began taking my daughter to my half-brothers' home and there they would sexually abuse her.

It took me six years to figure out what was happening. I started to lose this amazing little girl piece by piece. Each year she got worse. I eventually married a great person and over time, he pieced it all together with me. At twelve, my daughter disclosed everything. It was heart wrenching and at that time I had a toddler and had just had another baby.

We had my mother charged along with my half-brother. It has been a long road of court battles but well worth it. I could never have stayed strong without the support of my loving and patient husband as well as my therapist who volunteered her time and services at no cost. After the trial was over, I learned the laws and rights I had to go after the father of my daughter.

A lot has happened in the past couple of years, but I'm staying strong and moving on with my children and husband. In the end, the ones who are suffering are the people who committed these awful acts. My daughter is sixteen and a wonderful artist. Art has been her saving grace. As for me, I have moved on and will never have contact with my parents and siblings again. My husband and I will be opening a foster home in the near future for children who have been abused.

> *"The world breaks everyone, and afterward, some are strong at the broken places."*
> --Ernest Hemingway

Becoming the Woman My Mother Knew I Could Be

Jessica Brinkman

At age 21, I would already have experienced being a caregiver, a college student, an employee, a mother figure, and a depressed, lost person. It all started mid-September 2003. My mom was making her rounds as a mail carrier when she suddenly doubled up in pain. She knew something wasn't right. She had been to the doctors multiple times before this incident and was already being treated for this pain. The doctors weren't sure what was going on.

I was at work when this happened. I had never before called my mom while I was at work, so I'm not sure why I had the urge to do so on this day. When she answered, I could hear her crying. She said that she was on her way to the hospital. When she arrived, they took X-rays. Within hours the doctors knew her body was full of cancer. We had to wait two more weeks until we would know exactly what kind of cancer it was.

They called for a biopsy. My dad was with my mom through everything, but because my dad's job required him to travel, he had to miss the biopsy. I was sleeping on the hospital floor when my mom's biopsy was completed. I heard her screaming that she never wanted me to let them do that to her again. She had undergone a biopsy without being sedated. They dug their way to her liver to get a sample … all while my mom was awake.

This was torture for me. I was by myself and all I could see was my once-strong mom, lying in pain, begging me not to let them touch her again. She did not want to feel that pain anymore.

On September 24, our family's fear came true. The focus that day was supposed to be on my parents' anniversary; instead that turned out to be the day our mother was diagnosed with cancer. Cancer that was usually found in the joints of children was now found throughout my mother's body.

After the diagnosis, we knew the battle would begin. The pain my mother had felt weeks before the diagnosis was now explained, but the pain was nowhere close to being eased. The cancer was in her pancreas and liver, and because it was so far along, there was nothing that could be done. Another oncologist had a different theory, though. He said that there was one technique we could try, involving dropping the chemo treatment directly on the areas affected with cancer.

My mom tried this once. One time was all it took to realize she didn't want to live this way. She decided to not do the treatment again.

From then on, my mom was in and out of the hospital. I was still working at this time so my routine was to go to work, drive to the hospital, stay the night with her, and start over again in the morning. This is not a lifestyle that can be sustained.

I was blessed to have a boyfriend who could see the pain my family was in. He insisted that I quit my job and be available to care for my mom at all times. He supported me. Whether it was emotionally or financially, he was always there. Imagine dating someone for just two years and then taking on this responsibility. I cannot thank him enough for this; because of him, I was able to be with my family instead of at a desk worrying. This man was a blessing in my life.

Going to and from work was difficult enough, but can you imagine going to and from elementary school knowing that your mom is extremely sick? My younger brother was 10 at the time—old enough to know what was going on, but too young to really process it. My dad and I made it our mission to not only care for my mother but to keep my younger brother's life as stable as possible. School had to stay constant; his surroundings had to remain stable. He was already a shy and timid child. He did not need instability around him.

Before we knew it, Thanksgiving was approaching. It was then that my dad had to allow hospice to come in. Our original plan was for my father and me to care for my mom. She was such a strong person that she didn't like accepting help from others, but she could never turn my father or me away. This plan had to change when legally we couldn't provide my mom with the amount of morphine she needed unless hospice came in.

My dad gave up everything to care for my mom. He went on FMLA to be her full-time caretaker along with me. I will never forget him buying a giant dry erase board so he could keep track of all of her medications and when she took it. I saw the love he had for this woman. He would do anything for my mom. He was always there.

My mom was on a lot of pain medication and eventually she stopped eating. As time passed, she was less alert. About a week before she passed, all she could do was flutter her eyes at us. She would tell us how much she loved us; she knew what was happening to her.

My mom passed on December 6, 2003, not even two months after she was diagnosed. My mother was my best friend.

She was more than just a mom; she was a woman I looked up to.

While caring for my mom, I'd remained in college and was also dealing with severe depression and anxiety. My life was crumbling.

The depression and anxiety had started when I was 19. I was in a very unhealthy relationship with a lot of drinking and drugs. I was cheated on, put down, and played. I did some things I'm not proud of during this relationship.

I finally got the strength and brains I needed to walk away. It was a Friday that I left this man. On the following Tuesday, Cory the blessing that I talked about earlier, walked into my life. It took me three months to even agree to go on a date with Cory and another three months to make it official that we were dating. He stuck with me, though. Maybe that's why this wonderful man is still in my life today.

I was not a stable person at this point. I would cry on a drop of a dime, I constantly had anxiety attacks, it was hard for me to go to work every day, I had very little trust, and I had an excessive amount of hate. I had been through hell and back, and Cory voluntarily chose to go with me.

For instance, while my mom was sick, Cory came over to give my dad and me a break. As he sat with her, she gave him her wedding ring. She knew that he would be the man I'd be with for the rest of my life. I'm not sure if he or I knew that at the time, but my mom did. Nobody knew about her giving him the ring; it was a secret between the two of them.

Cory knew he wanted to propose before she passed but the day he was going to, there was a scare with my mom at the hospital. I ran around the house to get dressed quickly and head to the hospital. It was then that he grabbed me and started telling me how much he loved me. I was expecting another lecture from him because he knew I hadn't been eating or sleeping during this time. Instead, he proposed.

My mom pulled through and I went to the hospital with a ring and a fiancé. I was able to tell my mom that her daughter was getting married. I had already decided that we would get married on my mom's birthday. It would be a winter wedding. She was happy and knew that it was coming; she even said we should think about decorating with snowflakes because of the winter theme.

The wedding planning began, but it was hard to be happy and excited during such a sad time in my life. My mom was dying. After she passed away, the craziness started. Cory and I bought a house and were busy planning a wedding. My dad went back to work, and I became the mother figure to my 10-year-old brother. My life used to be about me, but now I had a child to get to and from school, to cook for and do homework with. It was like Cory and I already had a family started.

Because my dad took off work to care for my mom, he had to work hard to get the family financially steady again. He wanted to be there for my brother as much as possible, but he had to travel so much; it was difficult. My brother was a part of the wrestling team;

my dad and I both planned our schedules around his meets. There wasn't one that my dad or I missed. It's like this little boy grew up to be our heart and soul. He grew up knowing our struggles and understanding us. We couldn't be more proud of the man he is today.

After my mom's death, I took a job at our local clinic. The constant sight of white lab coats, nurses and surgeons sent my depression levels to new highs. I was diagnosed with post-traumatic stress disorder. I was on six medications at one time. I had medications that I would take regularly and medications I would take when I could feel something coming on. I had to see counselors, but that gave me more anxiety and depression because we couldn't afford it. I got to the point where I couldn't even work; I couldn't leave my bedroom without having a panic attack or crying. I knew I had a problem.

This went on for a couple of years. I think deep down, I knew that I was a good person with a good heart; I was just so full of medication that I was numb to the world and couldn't express those feelings. I felt like a freak, but I found an awesome doctor who helped me understand that I wasn't.

People who have not experienced anxiety or depression have no idea. You can't control what you think or do; it is a constant struggle against yourself. When you add in the extra pressures of planning a wedding, raising a child and trying to make a home, just getting out of bed seems impossible.

Cory fought for me to get better. He wanted me better, and I wanted to be better. I appreciated everything he did. Who knows if I would be where I am today without him. I was also fighting to get better for my younger brother. He already lost his mother; he did not need to lose his sister or see her struggling like this. I held on for my brother. He became my fight.

Little did I know that relief and recovery were around the corner. After my wedding, a great friend told me that her family had a business and she thought I would be good for a position they had open.

After thinking long and hard, I applied and was hired. I was still pretty messed up and full of problems at this point. I was down to four pills though, so I guess you could say this was an accomplishment. However, Cory was trying to talk me into going off all of my medicine.

I have no idea how it happened, or what provoked it, but my new boss and I had a three-hour heart-to-heart. It was then that I gained another support system. I now had the loving support of my husband at home and the growing support of my work family. With the help of my husband, coworkers and boss, I approached my doctors with the idea of going off my medication. They weren't pleased at first because they didn't know if I was ready, but they told me they would support my decision. They told me exactly what to do. I knew I was in for hell once again as I tried to wean my body from these pills that were acting as my lifeline.

I had anxiety attacks and breakdowns daily. I can remember getting to work, shutting my office door and just crying.

Times were hard, but I knew that I had my support systems. After I was off almost all of my medicine, I really had to face life. I could no longer live in the fog I was in before. I had to be me. I had one pill that I kept taking; I knew this was the pill that was making me function. But after losing my health insurance, I finally let it go. It was then that I could see how numb I was before. I could finally feel emotions. I was a real person again.

I am now completely off my medicine. I still have anxiety, but I am fighting each day to better myself. I used to have dreams each week of my mom passing away. A year ago those dreams stopped, and I finally had a dream of my mom in which she wasn't ill. I want to think that this is a sign that I am getting better as a person. I am the woman my mother knew I could be. I'm nowhere near perfect, but I work each day to get better.

Jessica Brinkman is a daughter, a wife, a sister and a friend. She is the office manager of an insurance agency in her hometown and enjoys traveling and spending time with her friends and family. Jessica is very involved with the local Relay for Life in her mother's honor as well as the Alzheimer's Association.

A single twig breaks,
but the bundle of twigs is strong.
--Tecumseh

My Eight-Year *Job* Journey

Bob Winberg

First, let me be clear on one point: I am only one of thousands of folks who suffer mental illness either as a direct or indirect consequence of physical and/or psychological abuse. Many of those people have suffered far worse injury than me.

Second, understand that I do not resent my parents or hold them accountable for my experiences as a child and adult. My parents were two damaged individuals themselves. They simply could not see or understand how their decisions and actions would have such devastating consequences for me.

My emotional problems began when I was three and a half years old. At that time my parents placed me in a children's home in Omaha, Nebraska, for about two months. I was left completely alone with only my teddy bear to protect me. I can still recall with clarity my frightened state of mind. It was then that my anxiety disorder was born. It was regularly encouraged by the circumstances I dealt with from that time forward.

My father was a federal narcotics agent and a very brave man. My mother was a homemaker. She suffered from paranoid schizophrenia, probably beginning in her early 20s. I believe this was partly attributable to the unspeakable abuse she endured as a child.

Our home was a place in which my mom's schizophrenia ran mostly unbridled. There is not sufficient time in this brief story to describe my experiences, but I do have one memory to share. When I was 10, my mother attempted to murder my half-brother, my father and me. In retrospect, it was only God's hand intervening at the last possible moment that changed the course of events. Although I am severely traumatized, I am alive today. After this event, there were no grief counselors and no one to turn to. I was expected to just stuff it down and go on.

My half-brother is five years older than I am. As children, we were polar opposites. A true Jacob and Esau comparison. I was of a gentle nature and my half-brother was a warrior. Next to my mom, he was my greatest nemesis growing up. Though I wanted to look up to him, that desire was crushed by his anger and mistreatment. I had nowhere to run and nowhere to hide from him. My home was a place that nurtured my anxiety disorder continuously.

On top of that, we moved from town to town, often moving multiple times in a single year. I was always an outsider. I never had any friends. For many, many months and years I was completely alone. As a result, I learned no social skills, something that I struggle with even today at 65 years old.

When I was four, my mom read the Bible to me every night before bed for about two or three consecutive weeks. She began with Genesis and we may have gotten as far as Exodus, Chapter 20. Not much progress or training had occurred, but, somehow, some way, God's word settled deep in my heart! The only other exposure I received was at public school, which in that era told the story of Jesus in Christmas plays.

Fast forward to when I was 14. I had burglarized a residence, stolen things and vandalized on several occasions. I was developing a juvenile record. However, when I learned that detectives were on my trail, I found myself at a crossroads. One night, I sat down at our kitchen table and made a vow to God that I would steal no more if He allowed me to escape punishment for the burglary. The detectives never showed up, which meant God had accepted my agreement.

Within a few short weeks my strength was tested when my friend stole a pickup truck and wanted me to go on a joyride with him. Should I get in or not? In my heart, I knew I had promised God, so I refused. Shortly after, my friend's father threw me out of his house. He told me to never come back and said I was "no good." So, I was alone again. No audible victory short of praise from God. Only loneliness. No church. Nothing.

I continued on my way completely unchurched and unsaved. By the time I turned 15, we had moved to another part of the city, and I went about a year without any friends. At 16, I could not find a job because I was so scrawny for my age. However, God worked in my life again and the manager of an ice rink decided to hire me although I had no experience and could not even ice skate! Only the Holy Spirit could have moved that manager enough to see me as an employee, but I was still oblivious to God. I worked at the skating rink for two years driving the Zamboni, sharpening skates, working the counter, cleaning the restrooms, and most of all gaining self esteem and confidence. I saved my wages and in 1967, when I was 17, I purchase a 1965 Mustang with all the bells and whistles. Still, though, I became the subject of jealousy and eventually lost all my friends and faced social isolation once again.

At 18, I started college at Portland State. On my very first chemistry test I scored a 58, and I held a C average in my health class—not looking too good for pharmacy school, right?

Fortunately, by God's grace, my chemistry professor had one lab he taught for only 20 students in a class of 300. I was one of those students, so he got to know me. Thanks to that lab, when my grades came out I got a B in chemistry! Overall, I had a 2.0 GPA. I had given up on the idea of college much less pharmacy school, but because I had some generous professors (including the speech professor who'd led me to believe that I would be failed but didn't fail me after all) I was able to realize my dream to become a pharmacist like my dad.

My next encounter with God occurred in April 1971, at the age of 20. Three of my fraternity brothers were involved in a serious car accident on the street behind our fraternity house. They had asked me to ride with them earlier, but I elected to study organic chemistry of all things! Had I chosen to ride, I very probably would have been killed. It was midnight, and I heard the squealing tires and explosion from the car hitting an oak tree. I ran out and didn't recognize the car. Somehow in the confusion that ensued, I wound up in the ambulance (actually a paddy wagon) with Scott, one of the fraternity brothers. I watched Scott die in the paddy wagon. Just me, Scott, and a police officer. In the ER, they worked feverishly with Scott. I turned to God and prayed for Him to save Scott's life, but it was not to be. To make matters more tragic, Scott was to be married the following Thursday to the girl who was pregnant with his baby.

While dealing with this tragedy, I had no counselors to talk to, no clergy, no one. I became very, very angry with God. I told my soon-to-be wife never to talk to me about God ever. I didn't want to have anything to do with Him!

I married in 1971, and graduated pharmacy school in 1973. On graduation day, no one from my family showed up. I received no cards from my family, as best I can remember. However, my wife and all of her family showed up for my graduation. I was very appreciative of their attendance; otherwise I would have had no one to celebrate with. They even bought me gifts, which I couldn't understand at all. No one had ever given me gifts for no reason and this seemed to be a "no reason" situation.

By age 25, I was a married father of one and the chief pharmacist at a hospital that was a major referral center for Central Missouri—unheard of for someone so young. But I was woefully unequipped for life, whether as supervisor at the hospital or anything else involving social skills. Spiritually, I had no exposure at all. I'd only ever attended church or synagogue one time, which had been an almost insignificant event in my life, but that doesn't mean God was.

When I was pharmacy director, I hired a man—let's call him Mike—as a staff pharmacist. He had moved to Columbia to start a church. Long story short, the Holy Spirit led me to Christ through Mike, and I was baptized January 6, 1980, but I upset two apple carts in the process. First was my wife. She had reluctantly gone along with this Christ thing mostly due to my pressure, probably hoping this would blow over and be just another phase I was going through.

The second apple cart was Mike. I had not followed Mike's game plan regarding salvation and the path one takes to the cross. For the record, I believed in my heart that following his prescription would mean I risked losing my wife and family. On top of those two stressors, my job responsibilities were growing greater and greater. I found myself completely overwhelmed. I was also taking an extremely intense theology course entitled "Master Life" at church. My wife resented it. The course lasted 39 weeks and involved training in all aspects of Christianity (Bible reading, scripture memorization, study assignments, prayer, devotions, etc.). Only five of nine people who'd initially signed up for the course, from a church of 500, finished it.

Then, one final event occurred that created the perfect storm: I received news that my mother had murdered my father. Over the next few weeks and months my world came crashing down.

I had to meet my half-brother after 12 or more years of no communication, bury my father, settle the estate, visit my mother in prison and find legal counsel for her. It went on and on. One day, in an instant, all the emotions and trauma I had stuffed down came flooding into my life. My anxiety disorder exploded with unrelenting panic attacks.

Suddenly and without letup, I had anxiety 24 hours a day. My bed sheets were soaked with sweat every night. My chest pounded painfully all day and all night. I lived on just two to three hours of sleep a night. There was no relief. Days turned to weeks, then months. People looked at me in horror. I couldn't eat anything. My weight dropped from 164 to 139. I was a skeleton. My wife was frustrated and angry with me. I was ashamed.

The generalized anxiety disorder threw me into an ever-deepening depression.

In desperation, I told my wife I needed to resign from my position as pharmacy director. Her only response was, "How are you going to make up the difference in salary?"

I went to my pastor and he recommended a Christian psychologist who was a church member. The psychologist turned out to be completely incompetent, to the point of failing to recognize the seriousness of my state of mind. I didn't know how much longer I could continue. I began to make contingency plans in the event of my death.

My wife was growing impatient and angry. In 1982, the morning after Thanksgiving, she told me she was tired of the stress and drove me to the state hospital for the mentally insane and told me to get out and admit myself. I went to the admission desk and was informed they were closed and I would have to go somewhere else. We drove to a hospital with an ER. I was admitted to the psych ward. I asked my wife for her forgiveness but was met only with silence.

While I was absent from work, Mike went to the administrators and told them he should be made director of pharmacy since I was crazy. Upon my return, Mike approached me, and he said he'd asked for and received God's forgiveness. He also wanted my forgiveness. Too weak and beaten, I only responded, "You have God's forgiveness; you don't need mine." Years later I did send him note that I forgave him. By then he had attained my former position as director of pharmacy.

By 1986, Mike convinced everyone at work that I was acting strangely. One evening I was pulled from the pharmacy and led into an office by two administrative folks. They explained that they thought I was unwell and had a bed reserved for me in the psych ward. It was the most humiliating experience of my life. I explained that I had a psychiatrist and I would confer with him. I resigned my position in disgrace and humiliation. At the same time I divorced my wife.

The divorce essentially stemmed from two major events. The first was my decision to follow Christ. That was followed closely with my struggle with anxiety and depression. The net result was that over a three-year period, my wife grew weary, becoming angrier (understandably) and frustrated. During one moment of anger, she said that part of her loved me and part hated me. I couldn't reverse that process, even though I desperately wanted to. I couldn't even attend the divorce hearing. I was crushed. I had exhausted every option possible and divorce was the last thing I wanted. We had tried counseling, my daughter had begged us to stop fighting, and I was faced with the inevitable—my wife didn't love me anymore.

I lost everything of importance in life. I gave my wife the house and car, both paid for so I knew my kids would never be homeless. For the sake of our kids, I gave full custody to my wife. I did not know if I would even survive.

I was in a very dark period from 1982 to 1990. I call these years my Job journey.

During my Job journey after the divorce, I reasoned that God had forsaken me. I would occasionally fall on my knees and cry out to the Lord, "Why? What had I done?" Then I would audibly declare that regardless of my circumstances, I would continue to believe in God the Father and Christ the Savior, even if I felt like God had abandoned me. Though I had no hope, no self-respect, no job, no dignity and no way out, I still chose to follow Christ.

For some time I was on the threshold of becoming a street person. It could have gone either way. Church attendance or affiliation had long since ceased. Any Christian contacts had long faded away or had become my harshest critics. But unlike Job (a true man of God), I sought refuge in any port in the storm.

When my seven-year-old daughter was diagnosed with lung cancer in 1988, I was completely beaten, defeated and broken. Late in 1989, I met a woman named Bonnie and was introduced to an unconditional love that was pivotal in my life. It was something I had never experienced before.

Since then, I have very gradually improved to where I am today, but even now I struggle greatly with depression and anxiety. Some periods of time are okay and others are hard. It's a never-ending battle. I could never endure another eight-year-long Job journey, and I hope I never have to. Because of my ongoing depression and anxiety disorder, I have limited energy to engage in church service. In the past, I had been an elder and even chairman of the elders, but the associated duties left me feeling used up, and I would have to pull back in order to regain my emotional footing. I held Bible studies on Wednesday evenings at our home for some time before we had a church building. Other times, I had to decline opportunities presented because of my low energy levels. However, God has been so faithful over the years, always providing a way for me to serve Him in simple ways, and I'm thankful to Him for the opportunity. In June of 2015, we plan to pull an RV trailer to Alaska with a message on the trailer about God's testimony on the sanctity of life. This is our way of glorifying God and I am so thankful once again. Who knows how many people will read it!

By faith, I believe and hope all is well with my soul through Jesus my savior. In homeless kits I randomly hand out to those on the street, I enclose a gospel of John. On it, I write: *If you put your faith and trust in Jesus, no matter what your outward circumstance, know it is well with your soul!*

DESIGNING YOUR LIFE

What would happen if you discovered you could do more than just live your life—you could *design* it? This book teaches you to harness the power of your subconscious and program it to help you live a happy life fitting your definition of perfection.

DESIGNING YOUR LIFE: ACTION GUIDE

These exercises help you master your subconscious, abolish negativity and raise self-esteem. This guide focuses on creative visualization and powerful affirmations to control your life's design and master your future.

DEVELOPING PERSEVERANCE

A combination of internal roadblocks are holding you back, preventing you from persevering. This book shows you how to break through these self-imposed obstacles to begin moving along your true path, taking you further than you ever thought possible.

DEVELOPING PERSEVERANCE: ACTION GUIDE

With this guide, you'll learn about the unique roadblocks you've designed for yourself and explore the thoughts, feelings and events that impact your ability to succeed.

YOU DESERVE TO BE RICH

If you're busy blaming your lack of wealth on upbringing, education and environment, you're missing out on learning how easy it is to get rich. This book teaches you to throw away the excuses and focus on the 12 steps to securing a future of financial success.

YOU DESERVE TO BE RICH: ACTION GUIDE

You deserve an ideal life. This workbook helps you get there by providing activities and strategies that explain the rules of greatness, help define your dreams and work to banish your fears.

UNLEASH YOUR MOJO

You already possess everything you need to be the person you want to be, you just have to access these powerful traits. In *Unleash Your Mojo*, you'll learn to recognize all the greatness inside you and discover how to put it to use and start living your ideal life.

UNLEASH YOUR MOJO: ACTION GUIDE

Each of us has power to succeed, yet many of us never tap into that power. Instead, we stagnate on the sidelines while others flash forward in life. This workbook gives practical tips, advice and exercises to advance you in your quest for authenticity and power.

THE POSITIVE EDGE

There's a secret behind living a happy, successful, fulfilling life: *positivity*. Learn how to overcome your tendency toward negativity, how to control your life and future, and how easy it is to improve your confidence and self-esteem.

SPARK: THE KEY TO IGNITING RADICAL CHANGE IN YOUR BUSINESS

A complete, step-by-step training program to help you become a high performer and higher earner. Learn how to rise to the top of your profession, position yourself as an expert and attract the abundance you desire.

DARE TO SUCCEED

Get the motivation and the information you need to rise to the next level of success! America's #1 Success Coach, Jack Canfield, has gathered together the top business minds in one powerful book. This guide contains their secret strategies to conquer the competition and bring ongoing abundance into your life.

VICTORY JOURNAL

The *Victory Journal* demonstrates the importance of writing down all of your daily wins. Inside you'll find exercises to help define your ideal self and create action steps to move closer to your goals.

HARNESSING THE POWER OF GRATITUDE

Recognize the positive energy moving through your day, and harness it with this undated journal. Filled with inspirational quotes to help you maintain the spirit of gratitude, it's an ideal tool for developing an enduring, powerful habit of thankfulness.

APPRECIATING ALL THAT YOU HAVE

This 365-day journal filled with inspirational quotes provides a safe space to write down the many things for which you're thankful. It's the perfect way to help shift your perspective and recognize the abundance of positive forces in your life.

Share Your Story of Perseverance

Each one of us has been through a difficult time in our life. If you would like to share your story of perseverance to help motivate and give strength to others, visit www.storiesofperseverance.com and click on "Submit Your Story."

Many of us long for a world filled with positive stories, individual endurance, and personal success. Therefore, our gratitude for those who have the courage to share their story and have positively influence our readers is unsurmountable.

If you are interested in sharing your story, but have questions you would like answered first, please contact Kate Cooper at KateCooperPII@gmail.com.

In addition to submitting your story of perseverance online, you can email it to Kate Cooper at the address above, fax it to (419) 782-0645, or mail it to:

Stories of Perseverance
ATTN: Kate Cooper
2014 Baltimore Street
Defiance, OH 43512

We look forward to reading—and sharing—your story of perseverance and success!

Made in the USA
San Bernardino, CA
17 April 2016